Appliqué Delights

100 IRRESISTIBLE BLOCKS
from Piece O'Cake Designs

Becky Goldsmith & Linda Jenkins

C&T PUBLISHING

Text and Artwork © 2004 Becky Goldsmith and Linda Jenkins

Artwork © 2004 C&T Publishing, Inc.

Publisher: Amy Marson

Editorial Director: Gailen Runge

Editor: Lynn Koolish

Technical Editors: Gailen Runge, Karyn Hoyt, Gael Betts, Helen Young Frost

Copyeditor/Proofreader: Stacy Chamness, Susan Nelsen

Cover Designer: Christina D. Jarumay

Design Director/Book Designer: Kirstie L. McCormick

Illustrators: Tim Manibusan and Becky Goldsmith

Production Assistant: Luke Mulks

How-to Photography: Luke Mulks

Published by C&T Publishing, Inc., P.O. Box 1456, Lafayette, California 94549

Back cover: *25 Block Quilt, Spring Spectacular!*

Library of Congress Cataloging-in-Publication Data
Goldsmith, Becky.
  Appliqué delights : 100 irresistible blocks from Piece O' Cake Designs / Becky Goldsmith and Linda Jenkins.
     p. cm.
Includes bibliographical references and index.
  ISBN 1-57120-229-3 (Paper trade)
  1. Appliqué–Patterns. 2. Patchwork–Patterns. 3. Quilting. I. Jenkins, Linda. II. Piece O'Cake Designs. III. Title.
TT779.G6294 2004
746.46'041–dc22
                          2003022425

Printed in China

10 9 8 7 6 5 4 3 2 1

Table of Contents

Dedication

We dedicate this book to women, all kinds of women! We are all different, unique, and special. Let's embrace who we are. Let's support each other. Let's make some great quilts that tell the world something about ourselves.

Acknowledgments

We offer a great big thank you to Lynn Koolish, our editor at C&T. In teaching us new things about writing a good book, she is helping us to be better authors. We appreciate it.

Our technical editor, Gailen Runge, makes sure that we get the details right. It would be nice to be perfect but we aren't! We are thankful to have Gailen double-checking us. Kirstie McCormick, this book's designer, has given *Appliqué Delights* its distinctive appearance. We love the cover that Christina Jarumay designed. Luke Mulks, the production assistant, kept the many ducks in a row, making the publication of this book smooth. We thank you all for your excellent efforts.

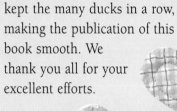

Introduction

This book actually began several years ago as a series of patterns. These little patterns were in the form of 25 different *Pin Pal Letters*. We loved the patterns but it was getting hard to keep up with the inventory, so we decided to print the next 25 patterns in the book *Dear Pin Pal*.

We just can't stop! We have added 50 brand new blocks to those first 50 blocks. There are now a grand total of 100 blocks all right here, in this book, plus we made new projects. If only there was more time . . .

The projects in this book are just a beginning! Use this book as a *block source book*. If you need a block for a particular project, flip through this book. These blocks are completely versatile; you can re-size them on a copier, and use them in any combination.

Here are some things to consider as you read this book:

❀ There are all kinds of blocks in this book. From flowers to chickens to fruit baskets and more—the variety of blocks will surprise you.

❀ Your quilts can evoke a bright and contemporary attitude or a more subdued Civil War manner depending on the colors you choose. Be creative! Make quilts that express the real you.

❀ You can make the blocks any size you like. The blocks are 5" x 5" but we give you instructions on how to enlarge the blocks up to 20" x 20".

❀ Don't be afraid to mix and match the blocks. The possible combinations are limitless.

We know you will find yourself coming back to these patterns, and this book, again and again.

Basic Supplies

Fabric: All of the fabrics used in these quilts are 100% cotton unless otherwise noted.

Thread: Use cotton thread with cotton fabric. There are many brands to choose from. Work with different brands until you find the one that works best for you. For hand appliqué we like both 50-weight DMC machine embroidery thread and Mettler 60-weight machine embroidery thread. For hand embroidery, we like one or two strands of Anchor or DMC floss. We also use perle cotton.

Batting: We prefer cotton batting. Our favorite is Hobbs Organic Cotton Batting.

Needles: For hand appliqué we use a size 11 Hemming & Son milliners needle. For hand embroidery the size 11 milliners needle works most of the time. If the thread is too big, try a fine crewel needle. There are many good needles. Find the one that fits *your* hand.

Pins: Use ½" sequin pins to pin your appliqué pieces in place. Use larger flower head quilting pins to hold the positioning overlay in place.

Fusible web: If you prefer to fuse and machine stitch your appliqué, use a paper-backed fusible web. For cotton use a light- or medium-weight fusible. Choose the one you like best and follow the directions on the package.

Non-stick pressing sheet: If you are doing fusible appliqué, a non-stick pressing sheet will protect your iron and ironing board.

Scissors: Use embroidery-size scissors for both paper and fabric. Small, sharp scissors are better for intricate cutting.

Rotary cutter, mat, and acrylic ruler: When trimming blocks to size and cutting borders, rotary cutting tools will give you the best results.

Pencils: We use either a General's brand white charcoal pencil or an Ultimate Mechanical Pencil for Quilters to draw around templates onto the fabric.

Permanent markers: To make the positioning overlay, an ultra-fine-point Sharpie marker works best on the upholstery vinyl.

Clear upholstery vinyl: Use 54"-wide clear medium-weight upholstery vinyl to make the positioning overlay. You can usually find it in stores that carry upholstery fabric.

Clear heavyweight self-laminating sheets: Use these sheets to make templates. You can find them at most office supply stores and sometimes at warehouse markets. If you can't find the laminate, use clear Contac paper.

Sandpaper board: When tracing templates onto fabric, place the fabric on the sandpaper side of the board. Then place the template on the fabric. You'll love the way the sandpaper holds the fabric in place when you trace.

Wooden toothpick: Use a round toothpick to help turn under the turn-under allowance at points and curves. Wood has a texture that grabs and holds.

Full-spectrum work light: These lamps give off a bright and natural light. A floor lamp is particularly nice as you can position it over your shoulder. Appliqué is so much easier when you can see what you are doing.

Quilting gloves: Gloves make it easier to hold onto the quilt during machine quilting.

Appliqué supplies

For Your Information

Fabric Preparation

Cotton has withstood the test of time and is easy to work with. We prewash our fabric before using it. This is a good way to test for colorfastness. Also, if the fabric is going to shrink, it does so before it is sewn into the quilt. The fabric is easier to work with, and smells and feels better if it is prewashed.

Fabric Requirements

Cotton fabric is usually 40" to 44" off the bolt. To be safe, we calculate our fabric requirements based on a 40" width.

Use the fabric requirements for each quilt as a guide, but remember that the yardage amounts will vary depending on how many fabrics you use and the sizes of the pieces you cut. Our measurements allow for both fabric shrinkage and a few errors in cutting.

Seam Allowances

All piecing is designed with ¼" seam allowances. Be accurate in your piecing so that your quilt tops will fit together properly.

The cutting instructions in this book are mathematically correct. However, variations in the finished size of your quilt top can result from slight differences in seam allowances and the amount of piecing. The measurements provided should be very close to your actual quilt size, but you should always measure *your* quilt and cut sashings and borders to fit.

Enlarging the Blocks

The blocks in this book are 5" x 5" square. You can use them this size or you can enlarge them. We admit it, neither of us is a math whiz. So when we realized how easy it is to enlarge a 5" block to the exact size we want, we were pretty proud of ourselves!

A 20% increase adds 1" to the block. For example, enlarge a 5" x 5" block by 120% and you get a 6" x 6" block. Every additional 20% adds one more inch to the block size. Remember to start with 100% so that you are enlarging and not reducing.

5" x 5" block x 120% = 6" x 6" finished size block
5" x 5" block x 140% = 7" x 7" finished size block
5" x 5" block x 160% = 8" x 8" finished size block
5" x 5" block x 180% = 9" x 9" finished size block
5" x 5" block x 200% = 10" x 10" finished size block

What if you want an even bigger block? Most copiers today will enlarge up to 400%. The problem is that the biggest paper in most copiers is 11" x 17". So if you want an 18" block, you need to enlarge the block in sections.

Begin by enlarging a 5" x 5" block to 10" x 10". Cut that block apart on the center lines to make four quadrants 5" x 5". Enlarge each quadrant by the percentage below to get the size you want. Tape the four enlarged copies together. Make sure that your center lines are straight and clearly visible. You may need to go over them with a ruler.

You will notice that as the block itself gets bigger, the widths of the lines get wider too. When making your overlay and templates aim for the center of these wider lines.

5" quadrant from 10" block x 110% = 11" x 11" finished size block
5" quadrant from 10" block x 120% = 12" x 12" finished size block
5" quadrant from 10" block x 130% = 13" x 13" finished size block
5" quadrant from 10" block x 140% = 14" x 14" finished size block
5" quadrant from 10" block x 150% = 15" x 15" finished size block
5" quadrant from 10" block x 160% = 16" x 16" finished size block
5" quadrant from 10" block x 170% = 17" x 17" finished size block
5" quadrant from 10" block x 180% = 18" x 18" finished size block
5" quadrant from 10" block x 190% = 19" x 19" finished size block
5" quadrant from 10" block x 200% = 20" x 20" finished size block

Stop! For correct information on producing these blocks, please refer to the inside front cover.

#1 Plumes

Special Techniques

Cutaway Appliqué: #1–#4
Circle Appliqué: #5, #6

#2 Petal Twirl

Special Techniques

Cutaway Appliqué: #1
Circle Appliqué: #4, #5

Refer to pages 88–92 for Special Techniques and pages 93–94 for Embroidery Stitches

#3 Spanish Flowers

Special Techniques

Cutaway Appliqué: #1, #7
Circle Appliqué: #4
Off-the-Block: #2–#4

#4 Honey Bee

Special Techniques

Cutaway Appliqué: #1, #2
Circle Appliqué: #6

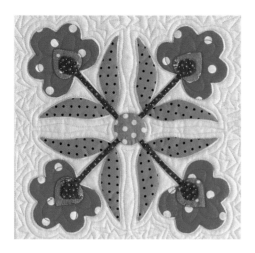

#5 Cotton Boll

Special Techniques

Cutaway Appliqué: #1, #4
Off-the-Block: #2–#3
Circle Appliqué: #5

Embroidery Stitches

Back Stitch: leaf veins

#6 Hooray Flower

Special Techniques

Cutaway Appliqué: #1, #2
Circle Appliqué: #7–#9
Off-the-Block: #7–#9

Embroidery Stitches

Random Straight Stitch: #4–#6, #8–#9
Back Stitch: flower pistils
French Knots: flower stamens

Refer to pages 88–92 for Special Techniques and pages 93–94 for Embroidery Stitches

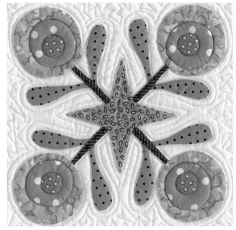

#7 Lollipop Flower

Special Techniques

Cutaway Appliqué: #1–#3, #7
Off-the-Block: #4–#6

#8 Plume Flower

Special Techniques

Cutaway Appliqué: #7, #8
Circle Appliqué: #9

Embroidery Stitches

Back Stitch: leaf veins

#9 Daisy Chain

Special Techniques

Cutaway Appliqué: #1
Circle Appliqué: #7–#9
Off-the-Block: #6–#8

#10 Petals and Points

Special Techniques

Cutaway Appliqué: #1, #2, #8
Circle Appliqué: #9, #10

Refer to pages 88–92 for Special Techniques and pages 93–94 for Embroidery Stitches

#11 Crossed Daisies

Special Techniques

Cutaway Appliqué: #1, #2
Circle Appliqué: #4

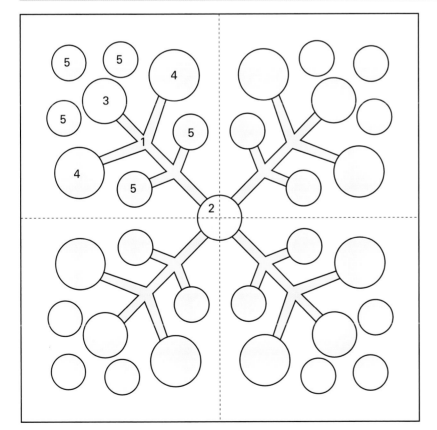

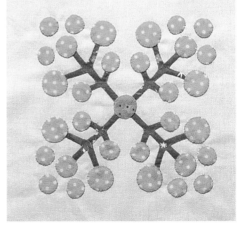

#12 Bubble Fun

Special Techniques

Cutaway Appliqué: #1
Circle Appliqué: #2–#5

Refer to pages 88–92 for Special Techniques and pages 93–94 for Embroidery Stitches

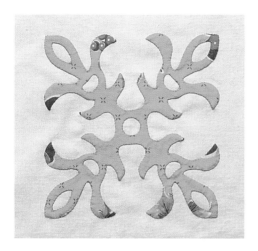

#13 Rorschach's (ink) Block

Special Techniques

Reverse Appliqué: #1–#3
Cutaway Appliqué: #4

#14 Oak Leaves

Special Techniques

Cutaway Appliqué: #1

Embroidery Stitches

Back Stitch: leaf veins

Refer to pages 88–92 for Special Techniques and pages 93–94 for Embroidery Stitches

#15 Tulip Whirl

Special Techniques

Cutaway Appliqué: #1

Embroidery Stitches

Chain Stitch: leaf veins, circles
Basket Weave: inside circles

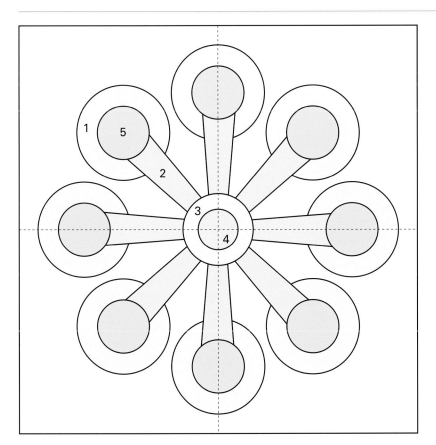

#16 Circular Logic

Special Techniques

Circle Appliqué: #1, #3–#5
Off-the-Block: #3–#4

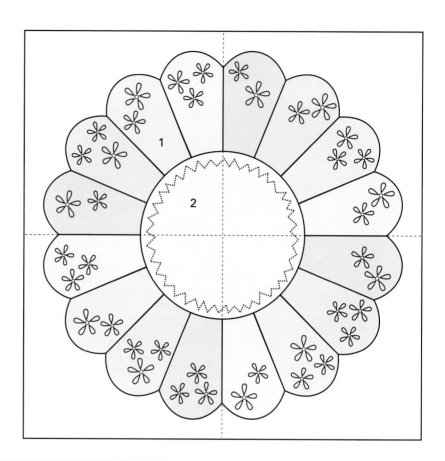

#17 Dresden Plate

Special Techniques

Circle Appliqué: #2

Embroidery Stitches

Zigzag Stitch: #2

Lazy Daisies: edge of plate

French Knots: daisy centers

#18 Rainbow Daisy

Special Techniques

Reverse Appliqué (done Off-the-Block):
   #2/#3

Embroidery Stitches

Random Straight Stitch: #2

Refer to pages 88–92 for Special Techniques and pages 93–94 for Embroidery Stitches

#19 Rose of Sherman

Special Techniques

Off-the-Block: #1–#3
Circle Appliqué: #3

#20 Sunflower

Special Techniques

Off-the-Block: #16–#17

Embroidery Stitches

Back Stitch: leaf veins
Random Straight Stitch: #17
Straight Stitch/French Knot Combination: #16
Blanket Stitch: #4–#15 after they are appliquéd

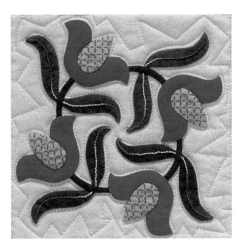

#21 Tulip Wreath

Special Techniques

Cutaway Appliqué: #1, #2

Embroidery Stitches

Back Stitch: leaf veins
Basket Weave: #4

#22 Flower Wreath

Special Techniques

Cutaway Appliqué: #1
Circle Appliqué: #8

Embroidery Stitches

Back Stitch: leaf veins
French Knots: #3–#7
Basket Weave: #8

Refer to pages 88–92 for Special Techniques and pages 93–94 for Embroidery Stitches

#23 Sunflower Wreath

Special Techniques

Cutaway Appliqué: #1
Circle Appliqué: #3, #4
Off-the-Block: #2–#4

#24 Cherry Laurel Wreath

Special Techniques

Cutaway Appliqué: #1
Circle Appliqué: #7

#25 Cherry Wreath

Special Techniques

Cutaway Appliqué: #1
Circle Appliqué: #5

Embroidery Stitches

Back Stitch: #4 leaf veins

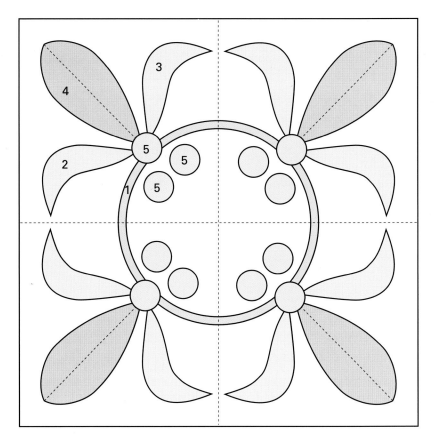

#26 Border Corner

Special Techniques

Circle Appliqué: #7, #8
Off-the-Block: #6–#8

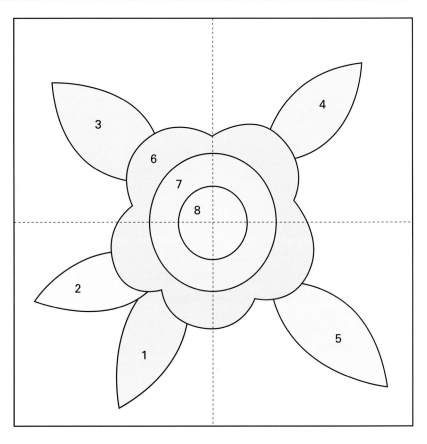

Refer to pages 88–92 for Special Techniques and pages 93–94 for Embroidery Stitches

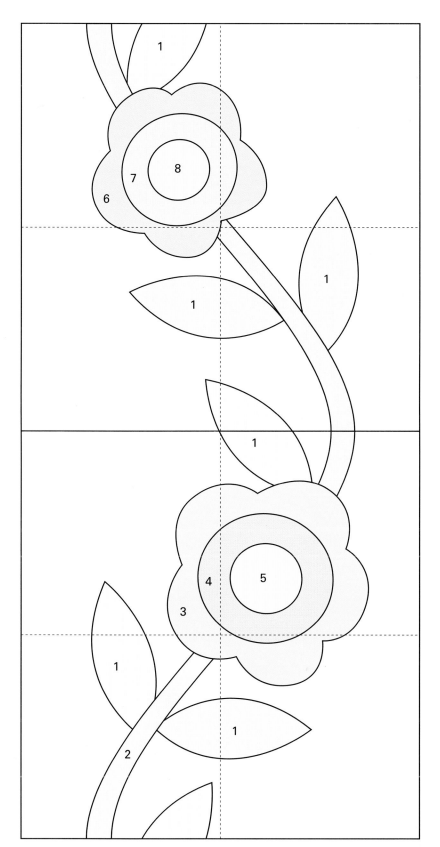

#27 and #28 Vine Border

Special Techniques

Bias Stem: #2
Circle Appliqué: #4, #5, #7, #8
Off-the-Block: #3–#5, #6–#8

#29 Flower Trio

Special Techniques

Cutaway Appliqué: #3, #5, #7
Circle Appliqué: #13, #14

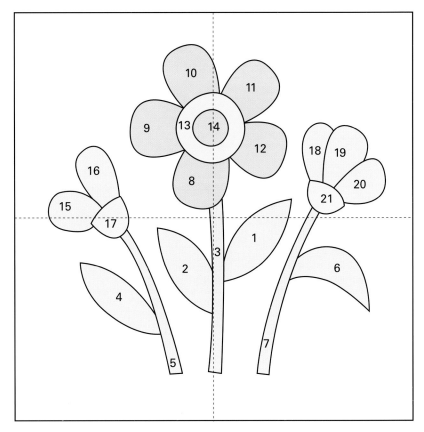

#30 Heart Flowers

Special Techniques

Cutaway Appliqué: #1–#5
Circle Appliqué: #7, #9

Refer to pages 88–92 for Special Techniques and pages 93–94 for Embroidery Stitches

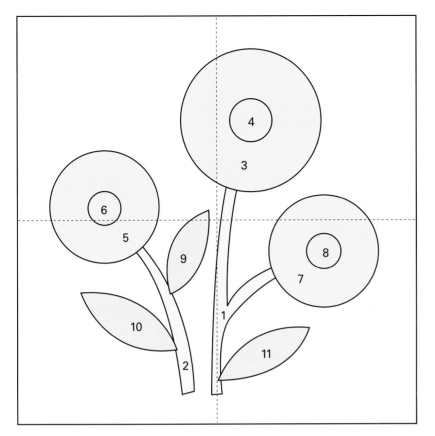

#31 Circle Flowers

Special Techniques

Cutaway Appliqué: #1, #2
Circle Appliqué: #3–#8
Off-the-Block: #3–#4, #5–#6, #7–#8

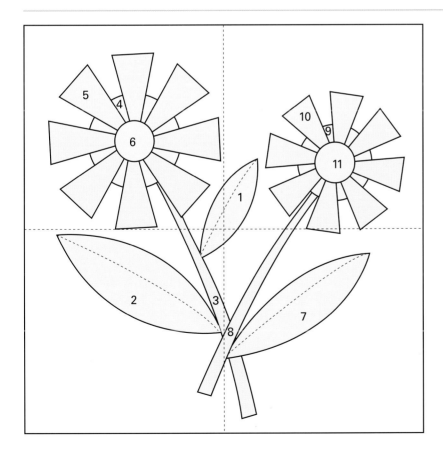

#32 Spoke Flower

Special Techniques

Cutaway Appliqué: #3, #8
Circle Appliqué: #4, #6, #9, #11

Embroidery Stitches

Back Stitch: leaf veins

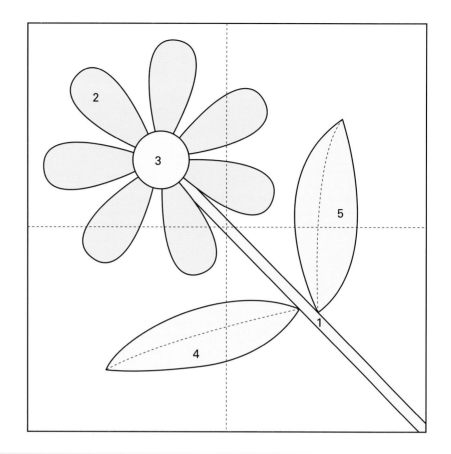

#33 Daisy

Special Techniques

Cutaway Appliqué: #1

Circle Appliqué: #3

Embroidery Stitches

Back Stitch: leaf veins

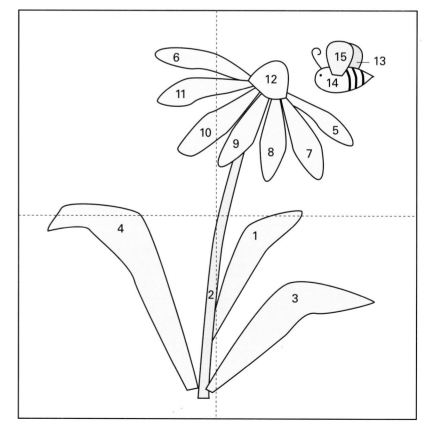

#34 Coneflower

Special Techniques

Cutaway Appliqué: #2, #5–#11, #13, #15

Embroidery Stitches

Back Stitch: bee's antenna

Black Gel Pen: Bee's eye and stripes

Refer to pages 88–92 for Special Techniques and pages 93–94 for Embroidery Stitches

#35 Flower Pot

Special Techniques

Cutaway Appliqué: #1
Reverse Appliqué: #7/#8

Embroidery Stitches

Back Stitch: leaf veins
Random Straight Stitches: #7
French Knots: #3

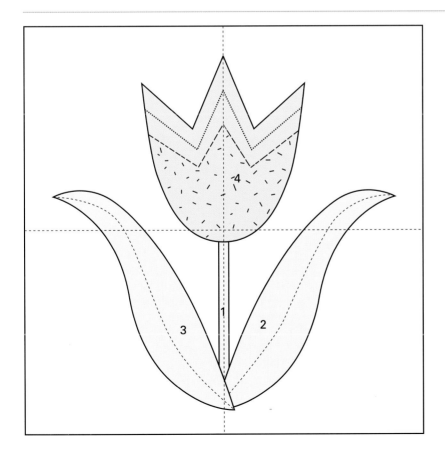

#36 Tulip

Special Techniques

Cutaway Appliqué: #1

Embroidery Stitches

Back Stitch: leaf veins
Random Straight Stitches: #4
Running Stitches: #4

#37 Pincushion Flowers

Special Techniques

Cutaway Appliqué: #1–#4
Circle Appliqué: #6–#11
Off-the-Block: #5–#8, #9–#11

#38 Diamond Flowers

Special Techniques

Cutaway Appliqué: #1–#3
Circle Appliqué: #5, #7

Refer to pages 88–92 for Special Techniques and pages 93–94 for Embroidery Stitches

#39 Two Flowers on a Stem

Special Techniques

Cutaway Appliqué: #1
Circle Appliqué: #5, #6, #8, #9
Off-the-Block: #4–#6, #7–#9

Embroidery Stitches

Back Stitch: leaf veins

#40 Star Flowers

Special Techniques

Cutaway Appliqué: #1–#10
Circle Appliqué: #11
Off-the-Block: #8/#11, #9/#11, #10/#11

#41 Vase of Flowers

Special Techniques

Cutaway Appliqué: #1–#6, #18, #21, #24
Circle Appliqué: #11, #13, #15, #17

Embroidery Stitches

Back Stitch: #27
French Knots: #27
Random Straight Stitches: #11, #13, #15, #17

#42 Basket of Flowers

Special Techniques

Cutaway Appliqué: #1–#8
Off-the-Block: #10–#12

Embroidery Stitches

Back Stitch: #9
French Knots: #9

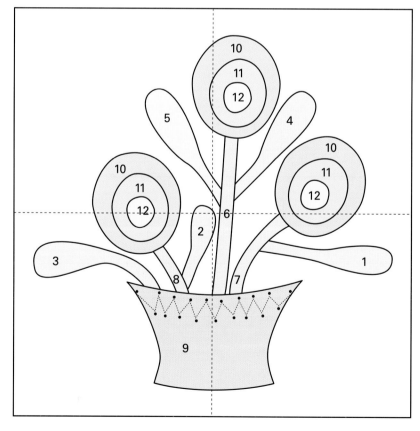

Refer to pages 88–92 for Special Techniques and pages 93–94 for Embroidery Stitches

#43 Fancy Flowers

Special Techniques

Cutaway Appliqué: #1, #7–#12
Circle Appliqué: #14–#16

#44 Medallion Vase

Special Techniques

Cutaway Appliqué: #1–#5, #8, #10,
  #17, #21, #43
Circle Appliqué: flower centers
Reverse Appliqué: #37–#39
Off-the-Block: #11–#14, #15–#16,
  #21–#22, #28–#29, #30–#32

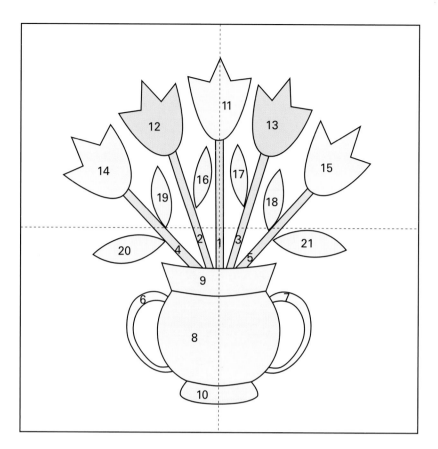

#45 Urn with Tulips

Special Techniques

Cutaway Appliqué: #1–#7

#46 Tulip Basket

Special Techniques

Cutaway Appliqué: #1, #3–#7

Embroidery Stitches

Simple Straight Stitches: "Xs" on #1 and #8.

Back Stitch: leaf veins, #8

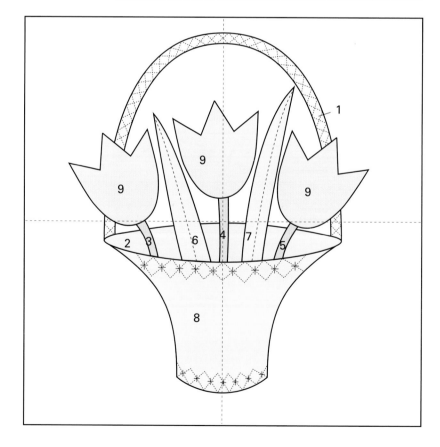

Refer to pages 88–92 for Special Techniques and pages 93–94 for Embroidery Stitches

#47 Urn with Flowers

Special Techniques

Cutaway Appliqué: #1–#7
Circle Appliqué: #9, #11, #12, #14

#48 Vase with Sunflowers

Special Techniques

Cutaway Appliqué: #4–#6, #8, #9
Circle Appliqué: #10, #11
Off-the-Block: #9–#11

#49 Apple Bowl

Special Techniques

Cutaway Appliqué: #5, #6
Circle Appliqué: #12

Embroidery Stitches

Back Stitch: leaf veins   Blanket Stitch: #9
French Knots: #9
Straight Stitch Flowers: #9

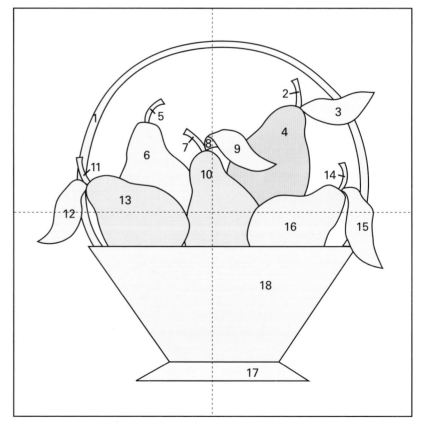

#50 Pear Basket

Special Techniques

Cutaway Appliqué: #1, #2, #5, #7, #8,
#11, #14, #17

#51 Pineapple

Special Techniques

Cutaway Appliqué: #1–#6

Embroidery Stitches

Back Stitch: leaf veins, #12

French Knots: #12

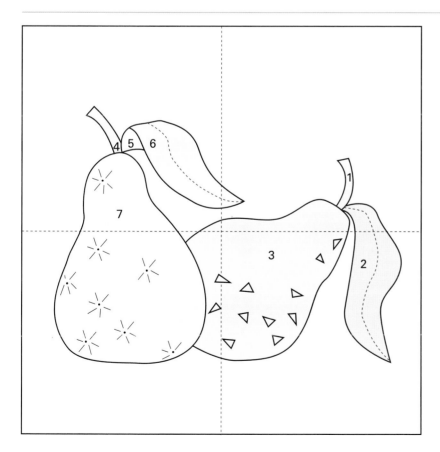

#52 Pears

Special Techniques

Cutaway Appliqué: #1, #4, #5

Embroidery Stitches

Back Stitch: leaf veins

Straight Stitch Triangles: #3

Straight Stitch Flowers: #7

French Knots: #7

#53 Strawberry Wreath

Special Techniques

Cutaway Appliqué: #1–#10

Embroidery Stitches

Back Stitch: leaf veins

Random Straight Stitches: #12

#54 Cherries

Special Techniques

Cutaway Appliqué: #2

Embroidery Stitches

Back Stitch: stems

Chain Stitch: leaf veins

Lazy Daisies: cherries

French Knots: cherries

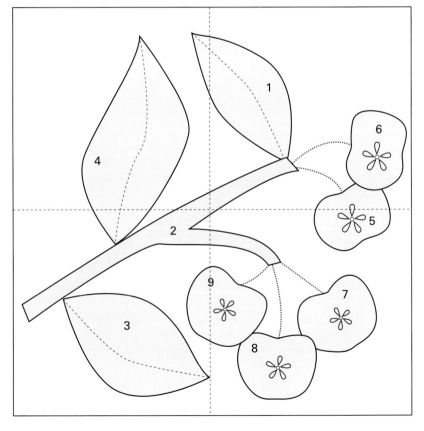

Refer to pages 88–92 for Special Techniques and pages 93–94 for Embroidery Stitches

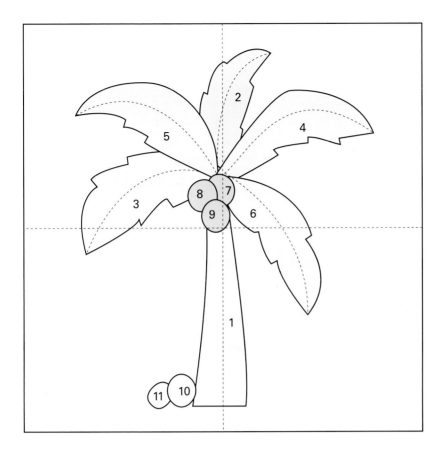

#55 Palm Tree

Special Techniques

Cutaway Appliqué: #11
Circle Appliqué: #7–#10

Embroidery Stitches

Back Stitch: palm leaf veins (optional)

#56 Apple Tree

Special Techniques

Cutaway Appliqué: #1, #2
Circle Appliqué: #3

Embroidery Stitches

Back Stitch: small branches

#57 Coffee Pot

Special Techniques

Cutaway Appliqué: #1–#5

Embroidery Stitches

Back Stitch: #1, #6
Blanket Stitch: #3
Bullion Knot on a Chain: #6
French Knots: #6

#58 Cup and Saucer

Special Techniques

Cutaway Appliqué: #1, #3, #4, #6–#8
Off-the-Block: #2–#3
Reverse Appliqué: #8 to #6 and #7

Embroidery Stitches

Back Stitch: #2, #5   Lazy Daisies: #5
Zigzag Stitch: #3, #5   French Knots: #5

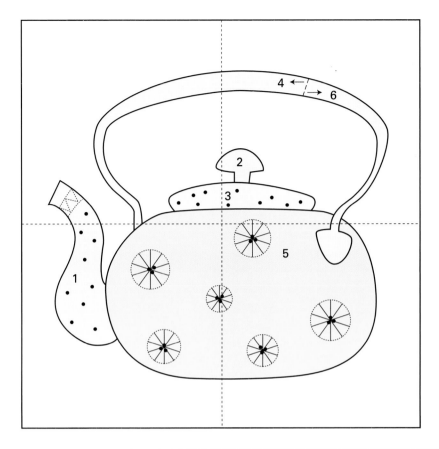

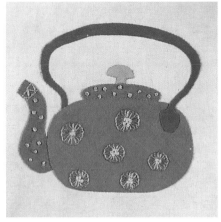

#59 Teapot

Special Techniques

Cutaway Appliqué: #1, #2, #4/#6

Embroidery Stitches

Back Stitch: #1
Zigzag Stitch: #1
Blanket Stitch Circles: #5
French Knots: #1, #3, #5

#60 Coffee Pot

Special Techniques

Cutaway Appliqué: #1–#4, #6–#9
Circle Appliqué: #10

Embroidery Stitches

Back Stitch: #5
French Knots: #5

#61 Teacup (A)

Special Techniques

Cutaway Appliqué: #2, #4

Embroidery Stitches

Back Stitch: #1

Chain Stitch: #1, #5

Lazy Daisies: #5

French Knot: #5

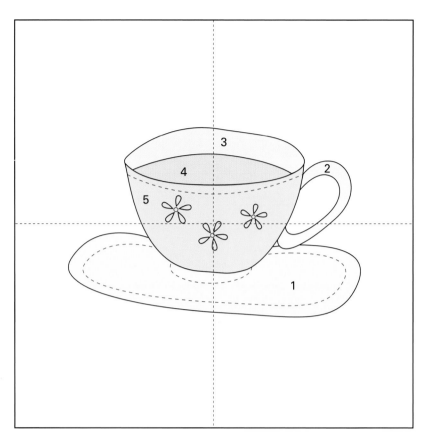

#61 Teacup (B)

Special Techniques

Cutaway Appliqué: #2, #4

Embroidery Stitches

Back Stitch: #1

Chain Stitch: #1, #5

Lazy Daisies: #5

French Knot: #5

Refer to pages 88–92 for Special Techniques and pages 93–94 for Embroidery Stitches

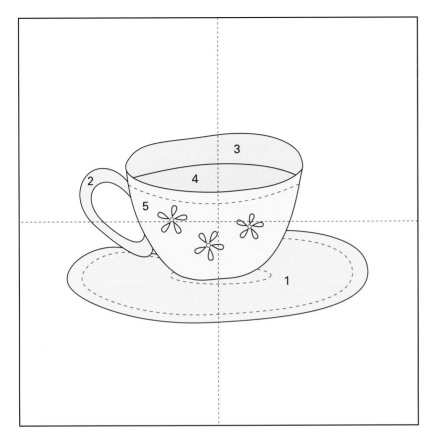

#61 Teacup (C)

Special Techniques

Cutaway Appliqué: #2, #4

Embroidery Stitches

Back Stitch: #1
Chain Stitch: #1, #5
Lazy Daisies: #5
French Knot: #5

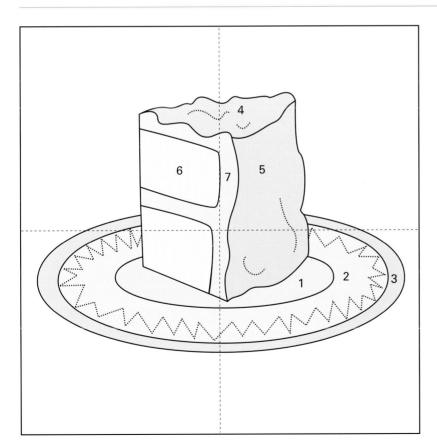

#62 A Piece O' Cake!

Special Techniques

Cutaway Appliqué: #2, #3, #7
Off-the-Block: #1–#3, #6–#7
Reverse Appliqué: #1, #2

Embroidery Stitches

Back Stitch: #2, #4, #5

Refer to pages 88–92 for Special Techniques and pages 93–94 for Embroidery Stitches

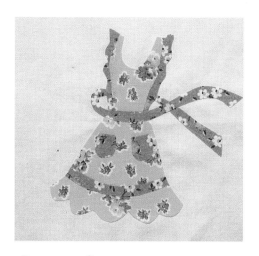

#63 Apron

Special Techniques

Cutaway Appliqué: #1–#4, #7–#10
Off-the-Block: #6–#9

#64 Alarm Clock

Special Techniques

Cutaway Appliqué: #1–#4, #8–#12
Circle Appliqué: #4, #5, #10
Off-the-Block: #4–#5

Embroidery Stitches

Back Stitch: #5

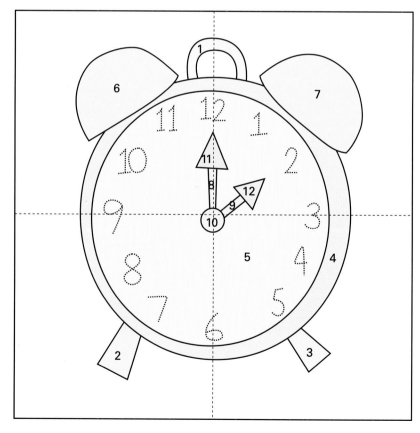

Refer to pages 88–92 for Special Techniques and pages 93–94 for Embroidery Stitches

#65 Telephone

Special Techniques

Couch the phone cord in place before you
stitch the appliqué.

Circle Appliqué: #4   Off-the-Block: #2–#4

Embroidery Stitches

Lazy Daisies: #2   Back Stitch: #3, #4
French Knots: #2

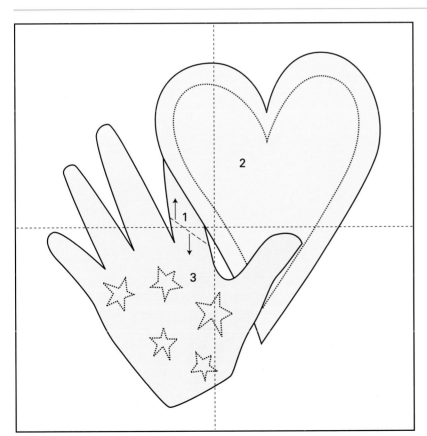

#66 Heart and Hand

Special Techniques

Cutaway Appliqué: #1/#3

Embroidery Stitches

Back Stitch: #2, #3

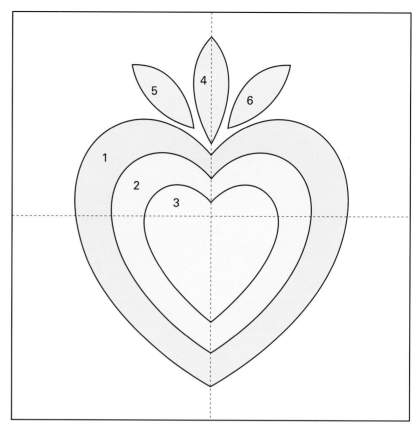

#67 Folk Art Heart

Special Techniques

Off-the-Block: #1–#3

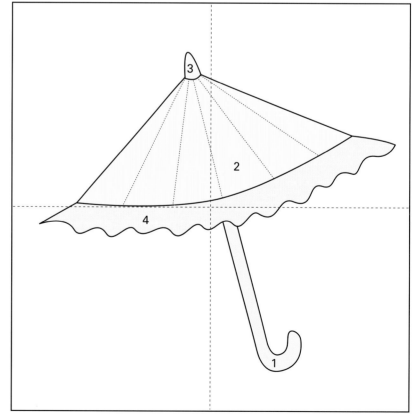

#68 Parasol

Special Techniques

Cutaway Appliqué: #1, #3, #4

Embroidery Stitches

Back Stitch: #2

Refer to pages 88–92 for Special Techniques and pages 93–94 for Embroidery Stitches

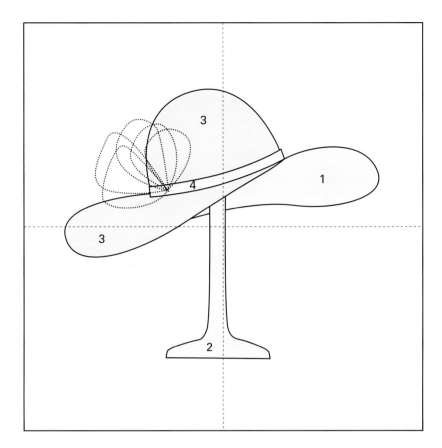

#69 Hat on a Hat Stand

Special Techniques

Cutaway Appliqué: #1, #2, #4

Embroidery Stitches

Optional: Use silk ribbon for the bow on the hat. Tack the loops in place with 1 strand of matching floss.

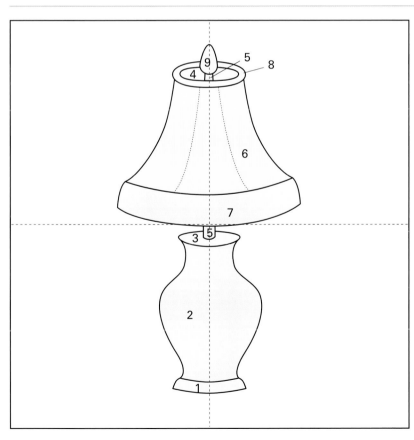

#70 Lamp

Special Techniques

Cutaway Appliqué: #1, #3–#5, #8, #9
Reverse Appliqué: #8 to #4/#5
Off-the-Block: #5 to #4

Embroidery Stitches

Back Stitch: #6

#71 Overstuffed Chair

Special Techniques

Cutaway Appliqué: #1, #10, #11

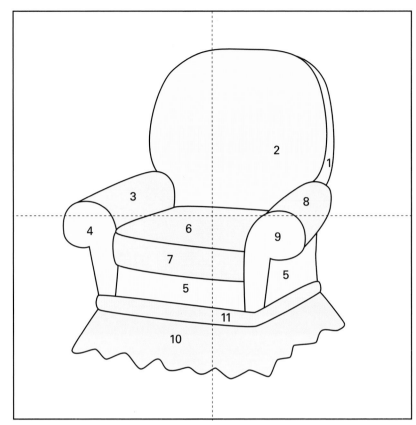

#72 Fancy Purse

Special Techniques

Cutaway Appliqué: #1, #6–#7
Circle Appliqué: #4–#5
Off-the-Block: #4–#5

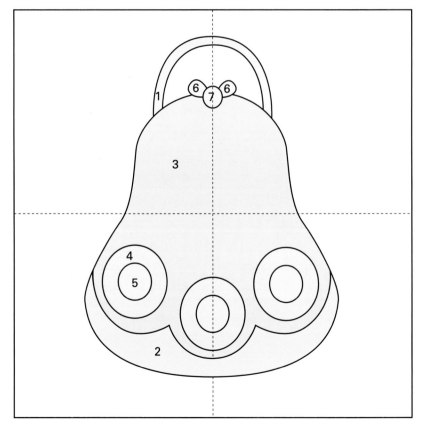

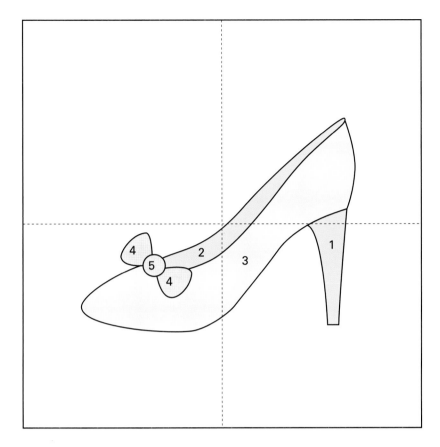

#73 Ladies' Shoe

Special Techniques

Cutaway Appliqué: #1, #2, #4
Circle Appliqué: #5

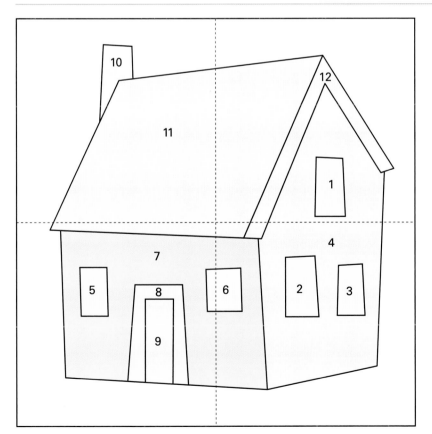

#74 Christy's House

Special Techniques

Cutaway Appliqué: #8, #12
Off-the-Block: #1–#4, #5–#7, #8–#9
Reverse Appliqué: #1–#3, #5, #6

#75 Mom's House

Special Techniques

Cutaway Appliqué: #5
Off-the-Block: #1–#3, #4–#5
Reverse Appliqué: #2, #3

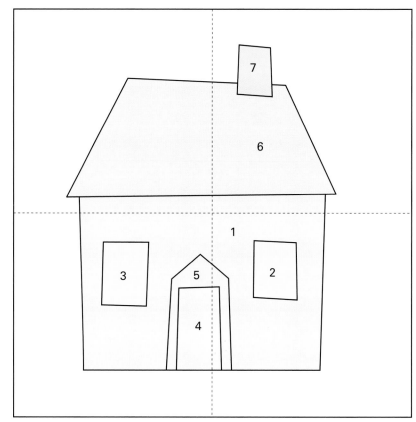

#76 Elanor's House

Special Techniques

Cutaway Appliqué: #4, #6, #8
Off-the-Block: #1–#3, #5–#6
Reverse Appliqué: #1, #2

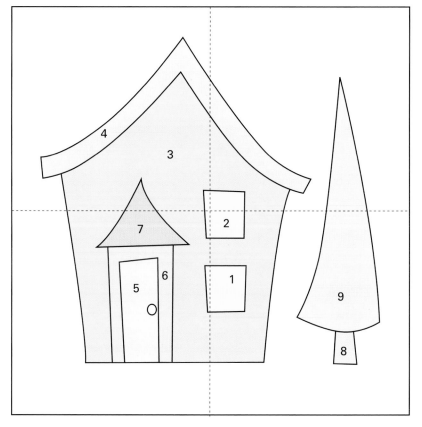

Refer to pages 88–92 for Special Techniques and pages 93–94 for Embroidery Stitches

#77 Becky's House

Special Techniques

Cutaway Appliqué: #5, #6, #8
Off-the-Block: #1–#3, #4–#5
Reverse Appliqué: #1, #2

Embroidery Stitches

Back Stitch: #1, #2, grass
Doorknob: cross 2 single stitches

#78 Butterfly

Special Techniques

Cutaway Appliqué: #9
Off-the-Block: #1/#5, #2/#6, #3/#7, #4/#8
Reverse Appliqué: #5–#8

Embroidery Stitches

Back Stitch: antenna, #5–#8
Blanket Stitch: #5–#8   French Knots: #1–#4

#79 Butterfly

Special Techniques

Cutaway Appliqué: #5

Embroidery Stitches

Back Stitch: antenna, #3, #4
Random Straight Stitches: #3, #4
French Knots: #1, #2, end of antenna

#80 Sunhat Sue

Special Techniques

Cutaway Appliqué: #1, #2, #4, #8, #9

Embroidery Stitches

Back Stitch: stems
Lazy Daisies: leaves and #3
Straight Stitch Flowers: bouquet, hat
French Knots: flower centers

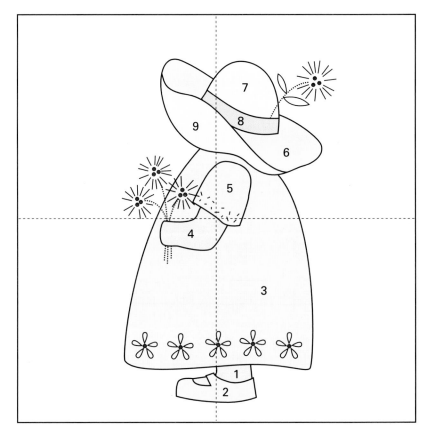

Refer to pages 88–92 for Special Techniques and pages 93–94 for Embroidery Stitches

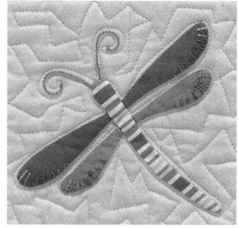

#81 Dragonfly

Special Techniques

Cutaway Appliqué: #1–#5

Embroidery Stitches

Back Stitch: antenna, #1–#4
French Knots: end of antenna

#82 Eggs

Special Techniques

Cutaway Appliqué: #1, #2

Embroidery Stitches

Back Stitch: legs and feet

Black Gel Pen: eyes

Refer to pages 88–92 for Special Techniques and pages 93–94 for Embroidery Stitches

#83 Chicken

Special Techniques

Cutaway Appliqué: #1–#6

Embroidery Stitches

Back Stitch: legs and feet, #7, #8

Black Gel Pen: eye

#84 Rooster

Special Techniques

Cutaway Appliqué: all pieces

Black Gel Pen: eye

Refer to pages 88–92 for Special Techniques and pages 93–94 for Embroidery Stitches

#85 Rise and Shine Chicken

Special Techniques

Cutaway Appliqué: #1–#6

Embroidery Stitches

Back Stitch: legs and feet

Black Gel Pen: eye

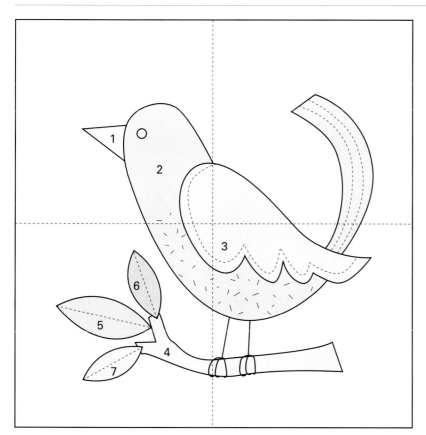

#86 Bird on a Branch

Special Techniques

Cutaway Appliqué: #1, #2, #4

Embroidery Stitches

Back Stitch: legs, feet, leaf veins, #2, #3
Satin Stitch: eye
Random Straight Stitches: #2

#87 Bird and House

Special Techniques

Cutaway Appliqué: #3, #4, #10
Reverse Appliqué: #1
Off-the-Block: #1–#2

Embroidery Stitches

Back Stitch: bird legs, #7, #9, #11
Lazy Daisies: flowers, roof trim
French Knots: eyes, daisy centers

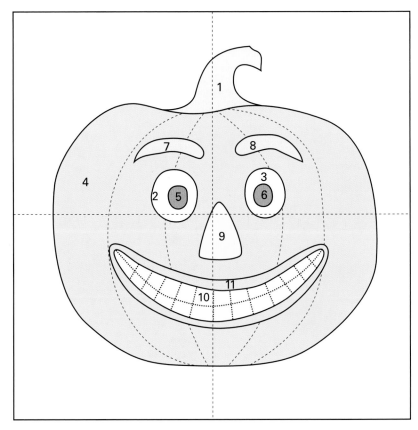

#88 Jack O' Lantern

Special Techniques

Cutaway Appliqué: #5–#8, #11
Circle Appliqué: #5, #6
Off-the-Block: #2–#3, #10–#11
Reverse Appliqué: #2, #3, #10

Embroidery Stitches

Back Stitch: #10, #4

Refer to pages 88–92 for Special Techniques and pages 93–94 for Embroidery Stitches

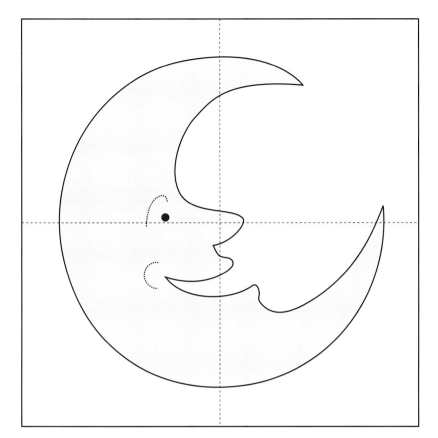

#89 Crescent Moon

Special Techniques

Cutaway Appliqué: moon

Embroidery Stitches

Back Stitch: cheek and eyebrow
Satin Stitch: eye

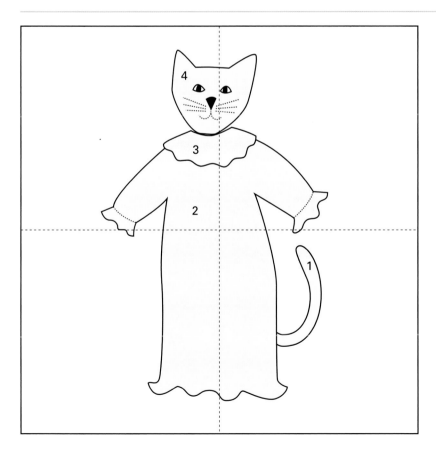

#90 The Cat's Pajamas (girl)

Special Techniques

Cutaway Appliqué: #1, #3, #4

Embroidery Stitches

Back Stitch: #2

Permanent Gel Pen: face

#91 The Cat's Pajamas (boy)

Special Techniques

Cutaway Appliqué: #1, #3, #6, #8, #9

Embroidery Stitches

Crossed Straight Stitches: #7

Permanent Gel Pen: face

#92 Cat

Special Techniques

Cutaway Appliqué: #1, #3, #4, #5, #7

Embroidery Stitches

Zigzag Stitch: #1
Back Stitch: #2, #6

Permanent Gel Pen: eyes

Refer to pages 88–92 for Special Techniques and pages 93–94 for Embroidery Stitches

#93 Ted E. Bear

Special Techniques

Cutaway Appliqué: #1–#3, #5–#8

Embroidery Stitches

Zigzag Stitch: #4

Back Stitch: #1, shoe laces

Permanent Gel Pens: face

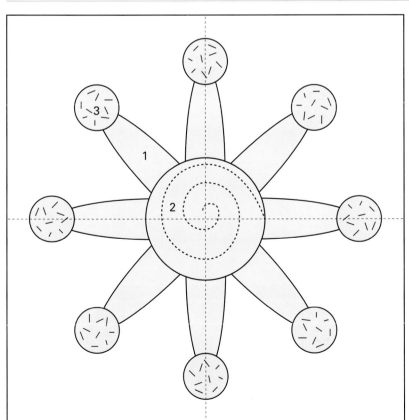

#94 Jester's Star

Special Techniques

Circle Appliqué: #2, #3

Embroidery Stitches

Back Stitch: #2

Random Straight Stitches: #3

#95 Snowflake

Special Techniques

Cutaway Appliqué: #1
Reverse Appliqué: center of #2

#96 Double Star

Special Techniques

Cutaway Appliqué: #1, #2
Circle Appliqué: #3
Off-the-Block: #1–#3

Refer to pages 88–92 for Special Techniques and pages 93–94 for Embroidery Stitches

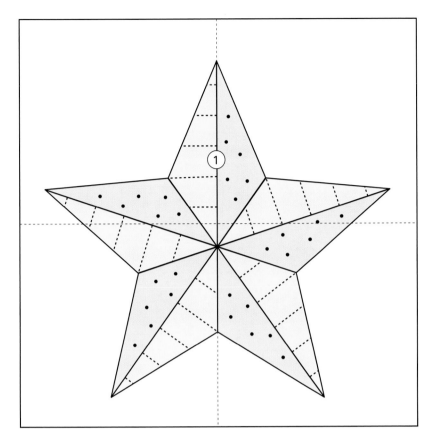

#97 Nautical Star

Special Techniques

Cut a light blue 1½" x 15" strip.
Cut a darker blue 1½" x 15" strip.
Sew them together.
Center the seam and cut #1 diamonds.

Embroidery Stitches

Back Stitch: light side   French Knots: dark side

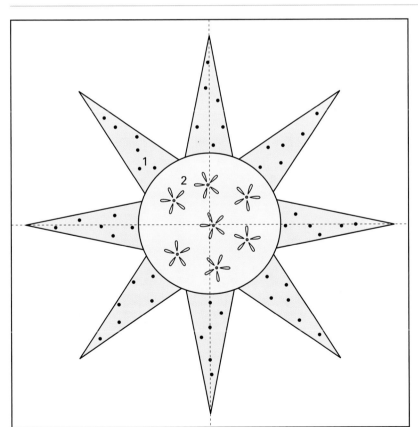

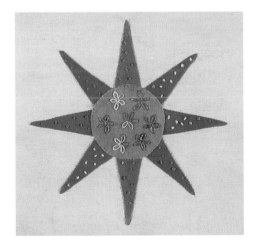

#98 Desert Sun

Special Techniques

Cutaway Appliqué: #1
Circle Appliqué: #2

Embroidery Stitches

French Knots: #1, #2
Lazy Daisies: #2

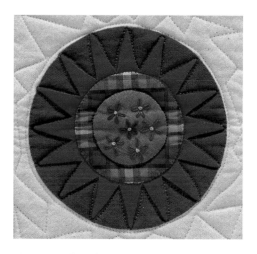

#99 NY Beauty

Special Techniques

Cutaway Appliqué: #2
Circle Appliqué: #1, #3, #4
Off-the-Block: #1–#4

Embroidery Stitches

Lazy Daisies: #4
French Knots: #4

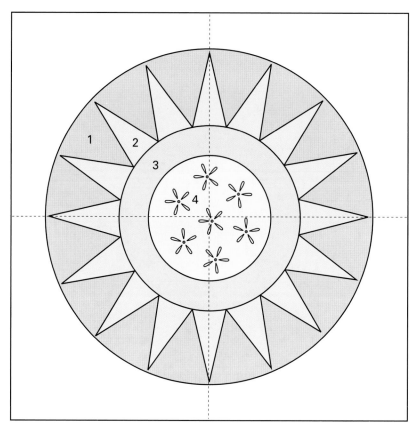

#100 Jeff's Sail Boat

Special Techniques

Sew the water to the background. Trim away the excess background fabric from behind the water, leaving a ³⁄₁₆" seam allowance.

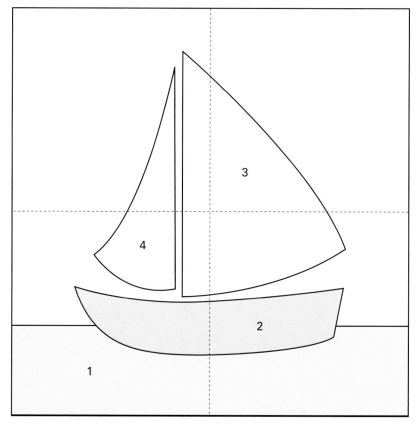

1-Block Mini Quilts

Made by Becky Goldsmith, 2003

Finished appliqué block size: 6" x 6"

Finished quilt size: 10" x 10"

Photos by Luke Mulks

1-Block Mini Quilts

Do you have a place for a grouping of small quilts? We'll bet you do. These quilts are quick and easy. Make one quilt, make more quilts! Keep them or give them as special presents to those you love.

Materials

Materials are for one mini quilt

Appliqué background: a fat quarter or large scrap

Appliqué: a wide variety of fabric scraps

Inner border: ⅛ yard or large scrap

Outer border: ⅛ yard or large scrap

Backing and sleeve: ½ yard

Binding: ½ yard

Batting: 14" x 14"

Cutting for Each Mini Quilt

Appliqué block fabric

Background: Cut 1 square 8" x 8".

Inner border fabric

A: Cut 2 strips 1" x 6½".
B: Cut 2 strips 1" x 7½".

Outer border fabric

C: Cut 2 strips 2" x 7½".
D: Cut 2 strips 2" x 10½".

Binding fabric

Binding: Cut 1 square 16" x 16" to make 2½"-wide continuous bias binding. (Refer to pages 90–91 for instructions.)

Cut fabric for appliqué as needed.

Block Assembly

Refer to page 5 for more information on enlarging a pattern. Refer to pages 83–86 for instructions on making the placement overlay and preparing the appliqué.

Appliqué Blocks

Becky used blocks #74, #75, #76, and #100, but you can use your favorites.

1. Enlarge the block by 120% to make a 6" x 6" pattern.

2. Appliqué the block. After the appliqué is complete, press the block on the wrong side. Trim the block to 6½" x 6½" square.

Appliqué Tips

Use the *cutaway appliqué* technique for the roofs and door jams, *reverse appliqué* for windows, and *off-the-block construction* as needed. (Refer to pages 88–90 for instructions.)

Quilt Assembly

Refer to the Quilt Assembly Diagram.

1. Sew an A inner border strip to each side of the block. Press seam allowances toward the inner border.

2. Sew 1 B strip to the top and 1 to the bottom. Press toward the inner border.

3. Sew a C outer border strip to each side of the quilt. Press seam allowances toward the outer border.

4. Sew 1 D strip to the top and 1 to the bottom. Press toward the outer border.

5. Finish the quilt. (Refer to pages 87 and 92 for instructions.)

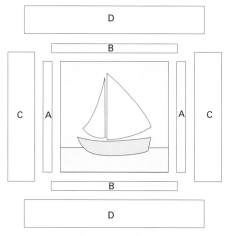

Quilt Assembly Diagram

Redwork Quilt

Designed by Linda Jenkins and Becky Goldsmith, made by Jane Green, 2001

Photo by Chris Marona

Finished embroidery block size: 5" x 5"

Finished quilt size: 19" x 25"

Redwork Quilt

Instead of appliquéing the blocks in this book, you can embroider them! Use red embroidery floss and a stem stitch and voila!—you have a redwork quilt. In fact, you can use any color of floss you like. Maybe a "purplework" quilt would suit you better!

Materials

Muslin backgrounds: ¾ yard

Red print sashing: ⅜ yard

Red mini-dot sashing corners: ⅛ yard

Backing and sleeve: ¾ yard

Binding: ⅝ yard

Batting: 23" x 29"

Red embroidery floss: 4 skeins

Cutting

Muslin fabric
Embroidery block backgrounds: Cut 12 squares 7" x 7".

Red print fabric
Sashing: Cut 31 strips 1½" x 5½".

Red mini-dot fabric
Sashing corners: Cut 20 squares 1½" x 1½".

Binding fabric
Cut 1 square 19" x 19" to make 2½"-wide continuous bias binding. (Refer to pages 90–91 for instructions.)

Block Assembly

Refer to pages 93–94 for instructions on embroidery stitches.

Embroidery Blocks

1. Choose any 12 blocks in this book. Make a copy of each chosen block. Tape 1 block copy onto your work surface so that it doesn't move.

2. Press the block backgrounds in half horizontally and vertically. Center a block background over the pattern. Tape the background fabric in place over the pattern. Lightly trace onto the fabric the lines to be embroidered. We use an Ultimate Marking Pencil for Quilters for this task. Repeat for all blocks.

3. Embroider the blocks. Jane used a back stitch in our quilt. After the embroidery is complete, press the blocks on the wrong side. Trim each block to 5½" x 5½" square.

Quilt Assembly

Refer to the Quilt Assembly Diagram.

1. Put the completed blocks on a design wall. Move them around until you are happy with their placement.

2. Sew 3 blocks together with 4 sashing strips between them. Press seam allowances toward the sashing. Make 4 rows.

3. Sew 3 sashing strips together end-to-end with 4 sashing corners. Press seam allowances toward the sashing. Make 5 rows.

4. Sew the 4 rows of blocks together with 5 rows of sashing between them. Press seam allowances toward the sashing.

5. Finish the quilt. (Refer to pages 87 and 92 for instructions.)

Quilt Assembly Diagram

25-Block Quilt

Made by Becky Goldsmith, 2001

Finished appliqué block size: 5" x 5"

Finished quilt size: 31" x 31"

Photos by Sharon Risedorph and Chris Marona

25-Block Quilt

*Mix and match 25 different blocks to make a cute little quilt. In fact, you might not be able to stop at 25! As you can see, Becky had to make **2** quilts!*

Materials

Appliqué backgrounds: 1⅛ yard of a single fabric or use a wide variety of fabric scraps

Appliqué: a wide variety of fabric scraps

Green mini-dot sashing: ½ yard

Green with white dot sashing corners and binding: ⅞ yard

Backing and sleeve: 1⅛ yard

Batting: 35" x 35"

Embroidery floss: as needed for selected blocks

Cutting

Block background fabric
Appliqué block backgrounds: Cut 25 squares 7" x 7".

Green mini-dot fabric
Sashing: Cut 60 strips 1½" x 5½".

Green with white dot fabric
Sashing corners: Cut 36 squares 1½" x 1½".
Binding: Cut 1 square 24" x 24" to make 2½"-wide continuous bias binding, (Refer to pages 90–91 for instructions.)

Cut fabric for appliqué as needed.

Block Assembly

Refer to pages 83–86 for instructions on making the placement overlay and preparing the appliqué. Refer to pages 93–94 for instructions on embroidery stitches.

Appliqué Blocks

1. Choose any 25 blocks in this book.

2. Embellish blocks with embroidery if you like.

3. Appliqué the blocks. After the appliqué and embroidery are complete, press the blocks on the wrong side. Trim each block to 5½" x 5½" square.

Appliqué Tips

Refer to pages 88–90 for instructions on special appliqué techniques as needed.

Quilt Assembly

Refer to the Quilt Assembly Diagram.
1. Put the completed blocks on a design wall. Move them around until you are happy with their placement.

2. Sew 5 blocks together with sashing strips. Press toward the sashing. Make 5 rows.

3. Sew 5 sashing strips together end-to-end with 6 sashing corners. Press toward the sashing. Make 6 rows.

4. Sew the 5 rows of blocks together with the 6 rows of sashing. Press toward the sashing.

5. Finish the quilt. (Refer to pages 87 and 92 for instructions.)

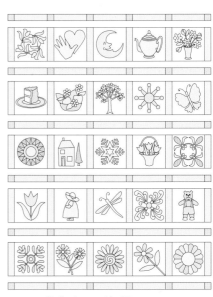

Quilt Assembly Diagram

Butterfly Garden

Made by Becky Goldsmith, 2000

Finished appliqué block size: 5" x 5"

Finished quilt size: 35" x 35"

Photo by Chris Marona

Butterfly Garden

Butterflies are amazing! Such beautiful clear colors arranged in intricate and delicate patterns – they float into the garden on a breeze. They remind us to stop for a moment and enjoy the beauty that is all around us.

Materials

Muslin backgrounds and inner border: 1⅞ yards

Appliqué: a wide variety of fabric scraps

Green mini-dot inner border: ⅜ yard

Green with white dot binding: ¾ yard

Backing and sleeve: 1½ yards

Batting: 39" x 39"

Embroidery floss: a variety of colors for antennae

Cutting

Muslin fabric

Appliqué block backgrounds: Cut 20 squares 7" x 7".
Appliqué border backgrounds: Cut 4 rectangles 7" x 27".
Checkerboard inner border: Cut 4 strips 1¾" x 40".

Green mini-dot fabric

Checkerboard inner border: Cut 4 strips 1¾" x 40".

Green with white dot fabric

Binding: Cut 1 square 24" x 24" to make 2½"-wide continuous bias binding. (Refer to pages 90–91 for instructions.)

Cut fabric for appliqué as needed.

Block and Border Assembly

Refer to pages 83–86 for instructions on making the placement overlay and preparing the appliqué. Refer to pages 93–94 for instructions on embroidery stitches.

Appliqué Blocks

1. Butterfly block #79 is used 16 times in this quilt.

2. Make a copy of the block and tape it to your work surface so it doesn't move.

3. Press the block backgrounds in half horizontally and vertically. Center a block background over the pattern. Tape the background fabric in place over the pattern. Lightly trace onto the block the antennae to be embroidered. We use an Ultimate Marking Pencil for Quilters for this task. Repeat for all appliqué blocks.

4. Appliqué the blocks. Embroider the antennae on each butterfly with a back stitch. After the appliqué and embroidery are complete, press the blocks on the wrong side. Trim each block to 5½" x 5½" square.

Appliqué Tips

Use the *cutaway appliqué* technique for the stems and butterfly bodies. Use the *circle appliqué* technique for the daisy centers. (Refer to pages 88–89 for instructions.)

Appliqué Border

1. Make a paper pattern for the border. Cut 1 piece of paper 5" x 25". The tulip in block #36 is used 5 times. Trace 1 tulip in the center of the border. Trace 2 tulips on either side of the first tulip. Space the centers 5" apart as shown below. Be sure to make a placement overlay from the paper pattern.

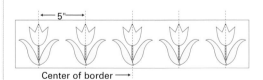

← 5" →

Center of border ⟶

Draw the border pattern.

2. Appliqué 4 borders. After the appliqué is complete, press the borders on the wrong side. Trim each border to 5½" x 25½".

Appliqué Border Corners

1. Block #33 is used 4 times for the border corners.

2. Appliqué 4 blocks. After the appliqué is complete, press the blocks on the wrong side. Trim each block to 5½" x 5½".

Checkerboard Inner Border

1. Sew the muslin and green 1¾"-wide strips together into pairs. Press toward the green. Cut 72 units 1¾" wide.

Sew strips together.
Cut 72 units 1¾" wide.

2. Sew 2 units together to form a square. Press toward the left. Make 36 squares.

Sew units together into squares.

3. Sew 8 squares together for the top and bottom checkerboards. Refer to the illustration below to make sure that you have the squares turned the correct way. Press toward the left. Make 2.

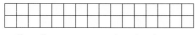

Sew 8 squares together for the top and bottom checkerboards.

4. Sew 10 squares together for the side borders. Refer to the illustration below to make sure that you have the squares turned the correct way. Press toward the left. Make 2.

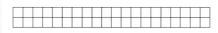

Sew 10 squares together for the side checkerboards.

Quilt Assembly

Refer to the Quilt Assembly Diagram

1. Put the completed butterfly blocks on a design wall. Move them around until you are happy with their placement.

2. Sew 4 butterfly blocks together into a row. Keep the angle of each butterfly the same. Press the seams in alternate directions so they nest when the rows are sewn together. Make 4 rows.

3. Sew the rows of butterflies together. Press the seams toward the bottom.

4. Sew the top and bottom checkerboards to the quilt. Change the direction of the seams in the checkerboards as necessary so they nest when sewn together, and re-press. Press the long seam toward the center of the quilt.

5. Sew a checkerboard to each side of the quilt. Change the direction of the seams in the checkerboards as necessary and re-press. Press the long seam toward the center of the quilt.

6. Sew the side borders to the quilt. Press toward the border.

7. Sew a daisy block to each end of the top and bottom borders. Be sure to position the daisy block as shown below. Press toward the corner.

8. Sew the top and bottom borders to the quilt. Press toward the border.

9. Finish the quilt. (Refer to pages 87 and 92 for instructions.)

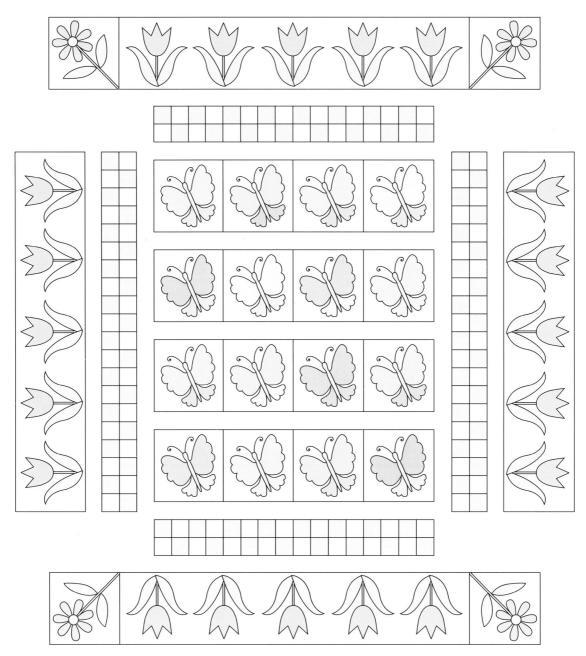

Quilt Assembly Diagram

Chicken Chase

Designed by Becky Goldsmith, made by Jane Green, 2000

Finished appliqué and pieced block size: 5" x 5"

Finished quilt size: 30" x 30"

Photo by Sharon Risedorph

Chicken Chase

Which came first—the plucky chicken or the determined little egg? We make no attempt to answer the question. But doesn't it make you wonder?

Materials

Black-and-white prints: 1¼ yard

Blue prints: a wide variety of fabric scraps to total at least ⅜ yard

Appliqué: a wide variety of fabric scraps

Backing and sleeve: 1⅛ yard

Binding: ¾ yard

Batting: 34" x 34"

Medium brown embroidery floss: one skein for the legs

Cutting

Black-and-white print fabrics
Appliqué block backgrounds: Cut 20 squares 7" x 7".
Broken Dishes blocks: Cut 8 squares 6¼" x 6¼", then cut twice on the diagonal to make 32 quarter-square triangles.

Blue print fabrics
Broken Dishes blocks: Cut 8 squares 6¼" x 6¼", then cut twice on the diagonal to make 32 quarter-square triangles.

Binding fabric
Cut 1 square 24" x 24" to make 2½"-wide continuous bias binding. (Refer to pages 90–91 for instructions.)

Cut fabric for appliqué as needed.

Block Assembly

Refer to pages 83–86 for instructions on making the placement overlays and preparing the appliqué. Refer to pages 93–94 for instructions on embroidery stitches.

Appliqué Blocks

1. Chicken block #83 is used 16 times in this quilt. Egg block #82 is used 4 times.

2. Make a copy of each block and tape to your work surface so they don't move.

3. Press the block backgrounds in half horizontally and vertically. Center a block background over the pattern. Tape the background fabric in place over the pattern. Lightly trace onto the block the legs to be embroidered. We use an Ultimate Marking Pencil for Quilters for this task. Repeat for all the appliqué blocks.

4. Appliqué the blocks. Embroider the chicken and egg legs using a back stitch. After the appliqué and embroidery are complete, press the blocks on the wrong side. Trim each block to 5½" x 5½" square.

Appliqué Tips

Use the *cutaway appliqué* technique for the beaks, combs, and tail feathers. (Refer to page 88 for instructions.)

Broken Dishes Blocks

1. Sew the black-and-white triangles and the blue triangles together into pairs. The edges that you will be sewing are on the bias so be careful not to stretch them. Press the seam allowances toward the blue triangle.

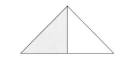

Sew triangles together into pairs.

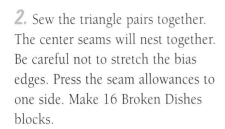

2. Sew the triangle pairs together. The center seams will nest together. Be careful not to stretch the bias edges. Press the seam allowances to one side. Make 16 Broken Dishes blocks.

Sew triangle pairs together to make 16 Broken Dishes blocks.

Quilt Assembly

Refer to the Quilt Assembly Diagram.

1. Sew 4 Broken Dishes blocks together. Turn the second and fourth blocks on their sides. Press seams toward the left. Make 2 rows.

2. Sew 4 broken dishes blocks together. Turn the first and third blocks on their sides. Press seams toward the right. Make 2 rows.

3. Sew the 4 rows together. Press seams toward the bottom.

4. Sew 4 chicken blocks together to make 2 side borders. Press the seams so they alternate with those in the center of the quilt. Sew the side borders to the quilt. Press seams to the border.

5. Sew 4 chicken blocks together for the top and bottom borders. Press seams so they alternate with those in the center of the quilt. Sew an egg block to each end of the top

and bottom borders. Press seams toward the center. Sew the top and bottom borders to the quilt. Press seams to the border.

6. Finish the quilt. (Refer to pages 87 and 92 for instructions.).

Quilt Assembly Diagram

Tea Time

Made by Linda Jenkins and Jane Green, 2000

Photo by Sharon Risedorph

Finished appliqué block size: 5" x 5"

Finished quilt size: 25" x 25"

Tea Time

*Do you remember your first tea party? We'll bet you were dressed to the max wearing a special hat and had a great time! Even if you don't drink tea, doesn't the **idea** of a tea party bring a smile to your face? Keep those happy times in mind with this cute quilt.*

Materials

Yellow appliqué backgrounds: 1 yard

Bright solid appliqué and sashing corners: a wide variety of fabric scraps

Yellow print sashing and outer border corners: ⅜ yard

Backing and sleeve: 1 yard

Binding: ⅝ yard

Batting: 29" x 29"

Embroidery floss: a variety of colors for teapots and writing

Cutting

Yellow fabric
Appliqué block backgrounds: Cut 9 squares 7" x 7".
Appliqué border backgrounds: Cut 4 rectangles 5" x 21".

Bright solid fabrics
Sashing corners: Cut 16 squares 1½" x 1½".

Yellow print fabric
Sashing strips: Cut 24 strips 1½" x 5½".
Outer border corners: Cut 4 squares 3½" x 3½".

Binding fabric
Binding: Cut 1 square 19" x 19" to make 2½"-wide continuous bias binding. (Refer to pages 90–91 for instructions.)

Cut fabric for appliqué as needed.

Block and Border Assembly

Refer to pages 83–86 for instructions on making the placement overlay and preparing the appliqué. Refer to pages 93–94 for instructions on embroidery stitches.

Appliqué Blocks

1. Teapot block #59 is used 9 times in this quilt.

2. To embellish each teapot with embroidery, lightly draw the designs you would like to use on your teapots. Use the photograph on the previous page as a guide and embroider using the stitches of your choice. Appliqué the blocks. After the appliqué and embroidery are complete, press the blocks on the wrong side. Trim each block to 5½" x 5½".

Appliqué Tips

Use the *cutaway appliqué* technique for the teacup handles. (Refer to page 88 for instructions.)

Appliqué Border

1. Make a paper pattern for each of the 4 borders. There are 3 different teacups in block #61: A, B, and C. The patterns for the words "tea time" and "time for tea" are on page 72. Cut 4 pieces of paper 3" x 19". Refer to the illustrations below and trace the appropriate teacups and words on the border papers. Be sure to make a placement overlay for each border.

Top border layout

Bottom border layout

Left side border layout

Right side border layout

2. Tape the top border pattern to your work surface. Center the border background fabric over the pattern. Tape the background fabric in place over the pattern. Lightly trace the words onto the borders you will embroider. We use an Ultimate Marking Pencil for Quilters for this task. Repeat for all borders.

3. Appliqué the borders. Embroider the words with a back stitch. After the appliqué and embroidery are complete, press the borders on the wrong side. Trim each border to 3½" x 19½".

Quilt Assembly

Refer to the Quilt Assembly Diagram.
1. Put the completed teapot blocks on a design wall. Move them around until you are happy with their placement.

2. Sew 3 teapot blocks together with 4 sashing strips. Press toward the sashing. Make 3 rows.

3. Sew 3 sashing strips together end-to-end with 4 sashing corners. Press toward the sashing. Make 4 rows.

4. Sew the 3 rows of blocks together with the 4 rows of sashing. Press toward the sashing.

5. Sew the side borders to the quilt. Press toward the sashing. Sew an outer border corner to each end of the top and bottom borders. Press toward the corner. Sew the top and bottom borders to the quilt. Press toward the sashing.

6. Finish the quilt. (Refer to pages 87 and 92 for instructions.)

tea
time

time for
tea !

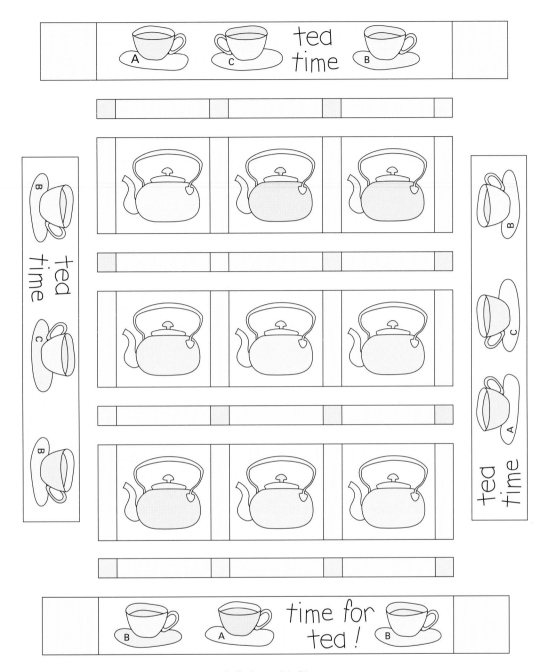

Quilt Assembly Diagram

Scrap Bag Surprise

Made by Linda Jenkins, quilted by Linda V. Taylor, 2003

Photo by Sharon Risedorph

Finished appliqué center medallion size: 18" x 18"

Finished small appliqué block size: 8" x 8"

Finished quilt size: 84" x 84"

Scrap Bag Surprise

*The simple piecing is a wonderful backdrop for the appliquéd flowers, showing off the cute designs in the printed fabric. Use **lots** of different fabric to make this happy, scrappy bed quilt.*

Materials

Center appliqué background: ⅔ yard

Checked tablecloth: ¼ yard

Off-white appliqué backgrounds: 1¾ yards

Appliqué: a wide variety of fabric scraps

Light piecing fabrics: a wide variety of fabric scraps to total at least 3⅞ yards

Dark piecing fabrics: a wide variety of fabric scraps to total at least 4¼ yards

Blue print sashing: ¾ yard

Red print sashing squares: a scrap at least 4" x 8"

Backing and sleeve: 7½ yards

Binding: 1⅛ yard

Batting: 88" x 88"

Cutting

Center appliqué fabric
Block background: Cut 1 rectangle 20" x 16¼".

Checked fabric
Tablecloth: Cut 1 rectangle 20" x 4¼".

Off-white fabric
Appliqué block backgrounds: Cut 24 squares 10" x 10".

Light fabrics
Four-Patch blocks: Cut 32 squares 3" x 3".
Square-in-a-Square blocks: Cut 384 squares 3½" x 3½".

Dark fabrics
Bars: Cut 32 strips 3" x 10½".
Four-Patch blocks: Cut 32 squares 3" x 3".
Square-in-a-Square blocks: Cut 96 squares 6½" x 6½".

Blue print fabric
Sashing: Cut 16 strips 1½" x width of the fabric.
Seam together as needed to cut:
    A. 2 strips 18½"
    B. 2 strips 20½"
    C. 4 strips 40½"
    E. 8 strips 8½"
    F. 4 strips 58½"

Red print fabric
Sashing squares D and G: Cut 8 squares 1½" x 1½".

Binding fabric
Binding: Cut 1 square 36" x 36" to make 2½"-wide continuous bias binding. (Refer to pages 90–91 for instructions.)

Cut fabric for appliqué as needed.

Block and Border Assembly

Refer to page 5 for more information on enlarging a pattern. Refer to pages 83–86 for instructions on making the placement overlay and preparing the appliqué.

Center Medallion

1. Sew the checked tablecloth fabric to the bottom of the background fabric. Press toward the tablecloth. Now press the square in half horizontally and vertically to establish the center grid.

2. Make a copy of block #44. Enlarge pattern 200% to 10" then cut the block into quarters. Enlarge each quarter by 180%. Tape the enlarged quarters together to make an 18" x 18" pattern.

3. Appliqué the center medallion. After the appliqué is complete, press it on the wrong side. Trim the center medallion to 18½" x 18½".

Appliqué Blocks

1. Enlarge blocks #29, #30, #31, #32, #37, #38, #39, and #40 by 160% to make an 8" x 8" pattern for each block.

2. Appliqué 2–4 of each block for a total of 24 appliqué blocks. After the appliqué is complete, press the blocks on the wrong side. Trim each block to 8½" x 8½".

Appliqué Tips

Use the *cutaway appliqué* technique for stems and small pieces and the *circle appliqué* technique for the flower centers. (Refer to pages 88–89 for instructions.)

Bars

1. Place 8 of the 3" x 10½" bars on each side of the center medallion as shown in the Quilt Assembly Diagram.

2. Arrange the 8 bars on each side until you are happy with their placement. Sew the bars together for each side of the center medallion.

Four-Patch Blocks

1. Use the 3" x 3" squares. Sew 1 light square and 1 dark square together. Press the seam allowances to the dark fabric. Repeat to make 32 pairs.

Sew squares together into pairs.

2. Sew 2 pairs together to make 16 Four-Patch block units. Press the seam allowances to one side.

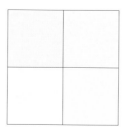

Make 16 Four-Patch block units.

3. Sew 4 Four-patch units together to make 4 Sixteen-patch block units.

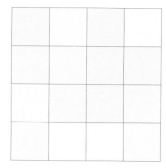

Make 4 Sixteen-Patch block Units.

Square-in-a-Square Blocks

1. Use the dark 6½" squares and the light 3½" squares. Sew 1 light square to 2 opposite corners of a dark square along a diagonal seam.

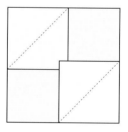

Sew squares to opposite corners with diagonal seams.

2. Trim away excess fabric leaving a ¼" seam allowance.

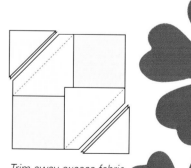

Trim away excess fabric.

3. Press the seam allowances toward the light fabric.

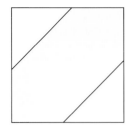

Press open.

4. Sew light squares to the remaining 2 corners of the dark square with a diagonal seam.

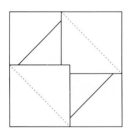

Sew squares to remaining corners with diagonal seams.

5. Trim away the excess fabric leaving a ¼" seam allowance.

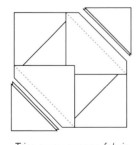

Trim away excess fabric.

6. Press seam allowances toward the light fabric. Repeat for all squares.

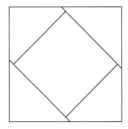

Press open. Make 96 blocks.

Quilt Assembly

Refer to the Quilt Assembly Diagram.

1. Sew A sashings to the top and bottom of the center medallion. Press toward the sashing. Sew B sashings to the sides of the medallion. Press toward the sashing.

2. Sew a bar unit to each side of the quilt. Press toward the sashing. Sew a sixteen-Patch block unit to each end of the top and bottom bar units. Sew the combined bar and sixteen-Patch block units to the quilt. Press toward the sashing.

3. Sew C sashings to the sides of the quilt. Press toward the sashing. Sew D sashing squares to both ends of the remaining C sashings. Sew the C/D sashings to the top and bottom of the quilt.

4. Sew the appliquéd blocks together for the sides. Sew an E sashing to the ends of the side appliqué sections. Press toward the sashing. Sew the side sections to the quilt. Press toward the sashing.

5. Sew 5 appliquéd blocks together for the top and bottom. Add E sashings, then the 2 outside blocks. Press toward the sashing. Sew the top and bottom sections to the quilt. Press toward the sashing.

6. Sew F sashings to the sides of the quilt. Press toward the sashing. Sew G sashing squares to both ends of the remaining F sashings. Sew the F/G sashings to the top and bottom of the quilt.

7. Sew the Square-in-a-Square blocks together in two strips, pressing seams in each strip in opposite directions so they nest when sewing the strips together. You will need 4 strips of 10 blocks each and 4 strips of 14 blocks each. Sew the strips together to form 2 sections of 20 blocks and 2 sections of 28 blocks.

8. Sew the 20-block sections to the sides of the quilt. Press toward the sashing. Sew the 28-block sections to the top and bottom of the quilt. Press toward the sashing.

9. Finish the quilt. (Refer to pages 87 and 92 for instructions.)

Quilt Assembly Diagram

Spring Spectacular!

Photo by Sharon Risedorph

Made by Becky Goldsmith, 2003

Finished appliqué block size: 8" x 8"

Finished quilt size: 50" x 50"

Spring Spectacular!

Spring is such a great time of year. The dull colors of winter give way to the fresh, bright, clear colors of spring! We love it — it's simply spectacular!

Materials

Off-white appliqué backgrounds: 2⅜ yards

Appliqué: a wide variety of fabric scraps

Yellow sashing and narrow bias accent strips:
   1¼ yards

Striped inner border and binding: ¾ yard

Backing and sleeve: 3¼ yards

Batting: 54" x 54"

Cutting

Off-white fabric

Appliqué block backgrounds: Cut 16 squares 10" x 10".
Appliqué border backgrounds: Cut 4 rectangles 7" x 42".
Appliqué border corner backgrounds: Cut 4 squares 7" x 7".

Yellow fabric

Sashing:
   A. Cut 12 strips 1½" x 8½".
   B. Cut 5 strips 1½" x 35½".
   C. Cut 2 strips 1½" x 37½".

Narrow bias accent strips: Cut 1 square 24" x 24" to make 1"-wide continuous bias. (Refer to page 90–91 for instructions.) Press the bias in half lengthwise, wrong sides together. Measure from the folded edge and trim the strip to ⅜" wide. Cut the trimmed bias into:
   F. 4 (folded) strips ⅜" x 40½"
   G. 4 (folded) strips ⅜" x 50½"

Striped fabric

Inner border:
   D. Cut 2 strips 2" x 37½".
   E. Cut 2 strips 2" x 40½".

Binding fabric

Binding: Cut 6 strips 2½" x width of the fabric. Sew strips together end to end. Press the strip lengthwise, wrong sides together.

Cut fabric for appliqué as needed.

Block and Border Assembly

Refer to page 5 for more information on enlarging a pattern. Refer to pages 83–86 for instructions on making the placement overlay and preparing the appliqué.

Appliqué Blocks

1. Enlarge blocks #2, #3, #4, #5, #7, #8, #9, #10, #11, #19, #23, #24, #43, #45, #47, and #48 by 160% to make an 8" x 8" pattern for each block.

2. Appliqué the blocks. After the appliqué is complete, press the blocks on the wrong side. Trim each block to 8½" x 8½".

Appliqué Tips

Use the *cutaway appliqué* technique for stems and small pieces and the *circle appliqué* technique for the flower centers. Make *continuous bias stem* for the stems in the border. (Refer to pages 88–92 for instructions.)

Appliqué Border

1. Blocks #27 and #28 are repeated to create the appliqué border. These blocks are not enlarged. Make 4 copies of these 2 blocks. Tape the copies together end to end as shown to make the paper pattern for the border. Delete the partial leaf at either end of the border. Be sure to make a placement overlay using the taped together paper pattern.

Make border pattern from 4 copies of blocks #27 and #28.

2. Appliqué the borders. After the appliqué is complete, press the borders on the wrong side. Trim each border to 5½" x 40½".

3. Block #26, the border corner block, is not enlarged. Appliqué 4 border corner blocks. After the appliqué is complete, press the blocks on the wrong side. Trim each block to 5½" x 5½".

Quilt Assembly

Refer to the Quilt Assembly Diagram.

1. Put the completed blocks on a design wall. Move them around until you are happy with their placement.

2. Sew 4 blocks together with 3 A sashing strips between them. Press toward the sashing. Make 4 rows.

3. Sew the 4 rows of blocks together with 5 rows of B sashing strips. Press toward the sashing. Sew a C sashing strip to each side of the quilt. Press toward the sashing.

4. Sew a D inner border strip to the top and bottom of the quilt. Press toward the inner border. Sew an E inner border strip to each side of the quilt. Press toward the inner border.

5. Baste an F narrow bias accent strip to the inside of all 4 borders.

6. Sew the top and bottom borders to the quilt. Press toward the inner border. Sew a border corner block to each end of the 2 remaining borders. Press toward the corner block. Sew a border to each side of the quilt. Press toward the inner border.

7. Finish the quilt. (Refer to page 87 for instructions.)

8. After you trim the edges of the quilt, baste the G narrow bias accent strips to the outer edge. Match the raw edges of the narrow bias accent strips to the raw edge of the top of the quilt. Sew the binding to the quilt over the narrow bias accent strips. (Refer to page 92 for binding instructions.)

Quilt Assembly Diagram

Appliqué Delights

General Appliqué Instructions

We have a great way to do appliqué using sturdy laminated appliqué templates and a clear vinyl positioning overlay that makes it a snap to position all the pieces. If you're new to Piece O' Cake Designs appliqué techniques, read through all of these instructions before beginning a project.

For a more complete description of all our appliqué techniques, refer to our book *The Appliqué Sampler.*

Preparing the Backgrounds for Appliqué

Always cut the background fabric larger than the size it will be when it is pieced into the quilt. The outer edges of the block can stretch and fray when you handle it while stitching. The appliqué can shift during stitching and cause the block to shrink slightly. For these reasons it is best to add 1" to all sides of the backgrounds when you cut them out. You will trim the blocks to size after the appliqué is complete.

1. Press each background block in half vertically and horizontally. This establishes a center grid in the background that will line up with the center grid on the positioning overlay. When the backgrounds are pieced, the seamlines are the grid lines, and you do not need to press creases for centering.

Press to create a centering grid.

Making the Appliqué Templates

Each appliqué shape requires a template, and we have a unique way to make templates that is both easy and accurate.

1. Use a photocopier to make 2–5 copies of each block. If the patterns need to be enlarged, make the enlargement as noted *before* making copies. Compare the copies with the original to be sure they are accurate.

2. Cut out groups of appliqué shapes from these copies. Leave a little paper allowance around each group. Where one shape overlaps another, cut the top shape from one copy and the bottom shape from another copy.

Cut out appliqué shapes.

3. Take a self-laminating sheet and place it shiny side down on the table. Peel off the paper backing, leaving the sticky side of the sheet facing up.

4. If you are doing hand appliqué, place the templates *drawn* side down on the self-laminating sheet. For fusible appliqué, place the *blank* side down. Take care when placing each template onto the laminate. Use more laminating sheets as necessary.

*Place appliqué shapes **drawn** side down for hand appliqué.*

*Place appliqué shapes **blank** side down for fusible appliqué.*

5. Cut out each individual shape. Try to split the drawn line—don't cut inside or outside of the line. Keep edges smooth and points sharp.

Cut out each template.

You'll notice how easy these templates are to cut out. That's the main reason we like this method. It is also true that a mechanical copy of the pattern is more accurate than hand tracing onto template plastic. As you use the templates, you will see that they are sturdy and hold up to repeated use.

Using the Templates for Hand Appliqué

For needle-turn (hand) appliqué, the templates are used right side up on the right side of the fabric.

1. Place the appliqué fabric right side up on a sandpaper board.

2. Place the template right side up (shiny laminate side up) on the fabric so that as many edges as possible are on the diagonal grain of the fabric. A bias edge is easier to turn under than one that is on the straight of grain.

3. Trace around the template. The sandpaper will hold the fabric in place while you trace.

Place templates with as many edges as possible on the bias and trace around each template.

4. If you are going to add embroidery to your block, it is better to embroider the appliqué piece now.

5. Cut out each piece, adding a ³⁄₁₆" turn-under allowance.

Cut out each piece adding a ³⁄₁₆" turn-under allowance.

6. Prepare the appliqué pieces for a block, and follow the instructions on the next page to make and use the positioning overlay.

Using the Templates for Fusible Appliqué

For fusible appliqué, templates are used with the drawn side down on the wrong side of the fabric. Use a non-stick pressing cloth to protect the iron and ironing board.

1. Follow the instructions on the fusible web and iron it to the wrong side of the appliqué fabric. Do not peel off the paper backing.

Iron fusible web to the wrong side of fabric.

2. Leave the fabric right side down. Place the template drawn side down (shiny laminate side up) and trace around it onto the paper backing of the fusible web.

Trace around template onto paper backing.

3. Cut out the appliqué pieces on the drawn line.

Cut out appliqué pieces on drawn line.

4. Prepare the appliqué pieces for a block, then follow the instructions on the next page to make and use the positioning overlay.

Making the Positioning Overlay

The positioning overlay is a piece of medium-weight clear upholstery vinyl that is used to position each appliqué piece accurately on the block. The overlay is easy to make and use, and it makes your projects portable.

1. Cut a piece of the upholstery vinyl, with its tissue paper lining, to the finished size of each block. Set the tissue paper aside until you are ready to fold or store the overlay.

2. Make a copy of the patterns in this book to work from. Enlarge as directed. Tape pattern pieces together as needed.

3. Tape the copy of a pattern onto a table.

4. Tape the upholstery vinyl over the pattern. Use a ruler and an ultra fine point Sharpie marker to draw the pattern's horizontal and vertical centerlines onto the vinyl.

Tape vinyl over pattern and draw centerlines.

5. Trace all the lines from the pattern accurately onto the vinyl. The numbers on the pattern indicate stitching sequence—include these numbers on the overlay.

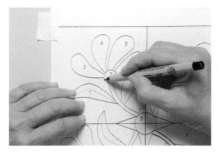

Trace pattern onto the vinyl.

Using the Positioning Overlay for Hand Appliqué

1. Place the background right side up on the work surface.

2. Place the overlay right side up on top of the background.

3. Line up the center grid of the fabric or the seamlines with the center grid of the overlay.

4. Pin the overlay if necessary to keep it from shifting out of position.

Place overlay on background and line up grids.

5. Before placing appliqué pieces on the block, finger-press the turn-under allowances. This is a very important step. As you finger-press, make sure that the drawn line is pressed to the back. You'll be amazed at how much easier this one step makes needle-turning the turn-under allowance.

Finger-press each piece with the drawn line to the back.

6. Place the first piece under the overlay but on top of the background. It is easy to tell when the appliqué pieces are in position under the overlay. As you work, finger-press and position one piece at a time. Be sure to follow the appliqué order.

Use overlay to position appliqué piece #1.

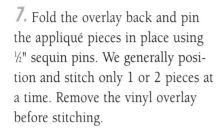

7. Fold the overlay back and pin the appliqué pieces in place using ½" sequin pins. We generally position and stitch only 1 or 2 pieces at a time. Remove the vinyl overlay before stitching.

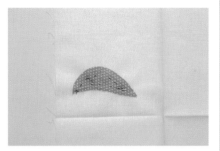

Pin appliqué piece in place.

8. Hand appliqué each piece in place with matching thread and an invisible stitch. Do not place and stitch more than 1 to 2 pieces at a time.

9. When you are ready to put away the overlay, place the tissue paper over the drawn side before you fold it. The tissue paper keeps the lines from transferring from one part of vinyl to another.

For Your Information

We don't trim the fabric behind our appliqué. We believe leaving the background intact makes the quilt stronger. And, should the quilt ever need to be repaired, it's easier if the background has not been cut.

Using the Positioning Overlay for Fusible Appliqué

1. Place the background right side up on the ironing board.

2. Place the overlay right side up on top of the background.

3. Line up the center grid of the fabric or the seam lines with the center grid of the overlay.

Place overlay on background and line up grids.

4. Peel off the paper backing from each appliqué piece before positioning it on the block.

5. Place the appliqué pieces right side up, under the overlay but on top of the background. Start with the #1 appliqué piece and follow the appliqué order. It is easy to tell when the appliqué pieces are in position under the overlay. You may be able to position several pieces at once.

Use overlay to position appliqué pieces.

6. Carefully remove the overlay and iron the appliqué pieces in place. Be sure to follow the instructions for your brand of fusible web. Do not touch the overlay vinyl with the iron because the vinyl will melt.

Fuse appliqué pieces in place.

7. After fusing cotton fabric, we sew the raw edges of the fused appliqué on the sewing machine using a straight or blanket stitch and matching thread. As the quilts are used, the machine stitching keeps the edges secure.

Pressing and Trimming the Blocks

1. Press the blocks on the wrong side after the appliqué is complete. If the ironing surface is hard, place the blocks on a towel and the appliqué will not get flattened.

2. Carefully trim each block to size. Measure from the center out, and always make sure the design is properly aligned with the ruler before you cut off the excess fabric.

Finishing the Quilt

1. Assemble the quilt top following the instructions for each project.

2. Construct the back of the quilt, piecing as needed.

3. Place the backing right side down on a firm surface. Tape it down to keep it from moving around while you are basting.

4. Place the batting over the backing and pat out any wrinkles.

5. Center the quilt top right side up over the batting.

6. Baste the layers together.

7. Quilt by hand or machine.

8. Trim the outer edges. Leave ¼" to ⅜" of backing and batting extending beyond the edge of the quilt top. This extra fabric and batting will fill your binding nicely.

Trim the outer edges.

9. Finish the outer edges with continuous bias binding. (Refer to pages 90 and 92.) Sew on any hard embellishments (buttons, beads, etc.) now.

Making a Label and Sleeve

1. Make a hanging sleeve and attach it to the back of the quilt.

2. Make a label and sew it to the back of the quilt. Include information that you want people to know about the quilt. Your name and address, the date, the fiber content of the quilt and batting, if it was made for a special person or occasion—these are all things that can go on the label.

Special Techniques

Cutaway Appliqué

The cutaway technique makes it much easier to stitch irregular, long, thin, very pointy or very small pieces. It is especially good to use for stems and stars.

1. Place the template on top of the selected fabric. Be sure to place the template on the fabric so that most of the edges will be on the diagonal grain of the fabric. Trace around the template.

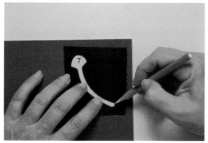

Place template with as many edges as possible on the bias and trace around the template.

2. Cut out the appliqué piece, leaving 1" or more of excess fabric around the traced shape. If you are working on a star or crossed stems, be sure to leave fabric intact between star points, the "V" between branches, and so on.

3. Finger-press, making sure the drawn line is pressed to the back.

4. Use the vinyl overlay to position the appliqué piece on the block.

5. Place pins ¼" away from the edges that will be stitched first. Place pins parallel to the edges. When a shape is curved, always sew the concave side first if possible.

Pin appliqué piece in place.

6. Begin cutting the excess fabric away from where you will start stitching, leaving a ³⁄₁₆" turn-under allowance. Never start at an inner or outer point.

Cut away excess fabric and begin stitching.

7. Trim away more fabric as you sew. Clip inner curves and points as needed.

8. Remove the pins as you stitch the next side of the piece. Clip away excess fabric as necessary.

9. Continue until all sides of the appliqué piece are stitched.

Reverse Appliqué

Use reverse appliqué when you want to cut through one piece of fabric to reveal the fabric below it.

1. Place the template with the opening in it on top of the selected fabric. Be sure to place the template on the fabric so that most of the edges will be on the diagonal grain of the fabric. Trace around the template.

2. In most cases, you will cut out the appliqué piece leaving 1" or more of excess fabric around it. Don't cut out the opening yet, but finger-press it, making sure the drawn line is pressed to the back. In our example, block #87, the reverse appliqué is stitched, then the outer edges of the design are stitched using the cutaway appliqué technique.

3. Position the appliqué piece on top of the fabric that will show through. Make sure that you leave the bottom fabric large enough to handle it easily. Pin the appliqué piece in place. Position the pins ¼" away from the edge that will be stitched first.

4. Cut inside the drawn line around the opening, leaving a ³⁄₁₆" turn-under allowance.

Pin appliqué in place and cut inside drawn line. Leave ³⁄₁₆" turn-under allowance.

5. Clip any inner curves or corners as necessary and begin sewing. Never begin sewing at a point or corner.

Begin sewing.

6. Finish sewing the opening.

Circle Appliqué

When sewing outer curves and circles you can only control one stitch at a time. Use the needle or a wooden toothpick to smooth out any pleats that form. Remember, the more you practice, the better you'll get.

1. Trace circles onto the selected fabric. Cut out each circle, adding a ³⁄₁₆" turn-under allowance.

2. Finger-press the turn-under allowance, making sure the drawn line is pressed to the back.

3. Use the vinyl overlay to position the appliqué piece. Pin it in place. Use at least 2 pins to keep the circle from shifting.

4. Begin sewing. Turn under only enough turn-under allowance to take 1 or 2 stitches. If you turn under more, the appliqué will have flat spaces and points.

Turn under only enough for 1 or 2 stitches.

5. Use the tip of the needle to reach under the appliqué to spread open any folds and to smooth out any points.

As seen from back. Use needle to open folds and to smooth points.

6. To close the circle, turn under the last few stitches all at once. The circle will tend to flatten out.

7. Use the tip of the needle to smooth out the pleats in the turn-under allowance and to pull the flattened part of the circle into a more rounded shape.

Finish stitching circle.

Off-the-Block Construction

It is sometimes easier to sew appliqué pieces together "off-the-block" and then sew them as a unit to the block. Use this technique when appliqué pieces are stacked one on top of the other as are the flower pieces in block #3.

1. Choose the fabrics that make up the appliqué. Trace around the templates onto the respective fabrics. Cut out the appliqué pieces leaving enough excess fabric around them so the pieces are easy to hold on to.

Trace and cut appliqué pieces.

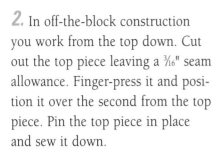

2. In off-the-block construction you work from the top down. Cut out the top piece leaving a ³⁄₁₆" seam allowance. Finger-press it and position it over the second from the top piece. Pin the top piece in place and sew it down.

Work from the top down.

3. Trim away the excess fabric from the newly created unit leaving a ³⁄₁₆" seam allowance. Finger-press it and position it over the next piece down. Pin the combined unit in place and sew it down.

Trim excess, position over next piece, sew in place.

4. Trim away the excess fabric from the flower unit leaving a ³⁄₁₆" seam allowance. It is ready to be finger-pressed and positioned on the block.

Finger-press and position on the block.

Making Continuous Bias

We find this method for making continuous bias to be particularly easy. A surprisingly small amount of fabric makes quite a bit of bias, and there is no waste. Use it for bias vines, as well as for bias binding. We show you how to master those tricky binding corners on page 92.

1. Start with a square of fabric and cut it in half diagonally.

2. Sew the two triangles together, right sides together, as shown. Be sure to sew the edges that are on the straight of grain. If you are using striped fabric, match the stripes. You may need to offset the fabric a little to make the stripes match.

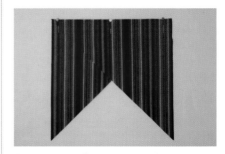

Sew straight-of-grain-edges of triangles together.

3. For bias for stems, press the seams to one side; otherwise press the seam allowances open. Cut the desired width into each side about 4" as shown.

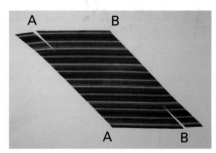

Cut desired width.

4. Match the A's and B's with the fabric right sides together. Pin and sew. Press the seam open.

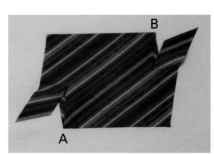

Pin and sew. Press.

5. Use a rotary cutter and ruler to cut the continuous bias strip to the desired width. Cut only 1 thickness of fabric as you work around the tube of fabric.

Cut to the desired width.

Cutting Tip for Continuous Bias

Try putting a small cutting mat on the end of the ironing board. Slide the tube of fabric over the mat. Use a ruler and rotary cutter to cut a long strip of continuous bias, rotating the tube of fabric as needed.

Cut using gentle pressure—if the ironing board is padded, the cutting surface may give if you press very hard.

Making Bias Stems

1. Make a continuous bias strip 1½" wide. (Refer to previous page for instructions.) Press the strip in half lengthwise with the wrong sides together.

Press strip in half lengthwise.

2. Place the folded edge of the bias strip along the correct line on the seam guide of the sewing machine (for ¼" stems use the ¼" line). Before you sew too far, insert the bias bar into the open end to make sure it fits. Sew the length of the bias strip.

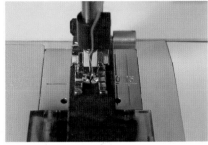
Sew using the sewing machine seam guide.

3. Trim away the excess fabric, leaving a very scant seam allowance.

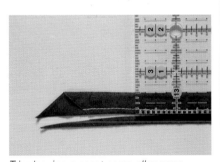
Trim leaving a scant seam allowance.

4. Insert the appropriate size bias bar into the sewn bias tube. Shift the seam to the back of the bar and press it in place. Move the bias bar down the tube, pressing as you go.

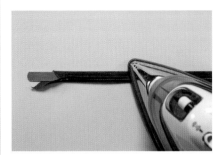
Press using the bias bar.

5. Hold up the finished bias stem. Notice that it curves more in one direction than the other. The side closest to the seamline makes the tighter curve. When possible, match this side of the bias stem to the concave side of the stem on the pattern.

Notice the direction of the curve.

6. This technique can be used for any width bias stem.

Making Fusible Bias Stems

Here's the best way to make bias stems if you prefer to do machine appliqué using fusible web.

1. Cut 6"-wide bias strips from the vine or stem fabric.

2. Iron 6"-wide strips of paper-backed fusible web to the back of the fabric.

3. Cut ¼"–⅜" strips for the stems or vines.

4. Peel away the paper backing and position stems on the block. Overlap the ends of the stems or vines as needed. When possible, place the end of the bias stem under a flower or leaf.

Sewing Binding to the Quilt

1. Cut the first end of the binding at a 45° angle. Turn this end under ¼" and press.

2. Press the continuous binding strip in half lengthwise, wrong sides together.

3. With raw edges even, pin the binding to the edge of the quilt front beginning a few inches away from a corner. Start sewing 6" from the beginning of the binding strip, using a ¼" seam allowance.

4. Stop ¼" away from the corner and backstitch several stitches.

Stop ¼" away from corner. Backstitch.

5. Fold the binding straight up as shown. Note the 45° angle.

Fold binding up.

6. Fold the binding straight down and begin sewing the next side of the quilt.

Fold binding down and begin sewing.

7. Sew the binding to all sides of the quilt, following the process above for the corners. Stop a few inches before you reach the beginning of the binding, but don't trim the excess binding yet.

8. Overlap the ends of the binding and cut the second end at a 45° angle. Be sure to cut the binding long enough so the cut end is covered completely by the turned-under end.

9. Slip the end that is cut at 45° into the turned-under end.

Slip 45° end into turned-under end.

10. Pin the joined ends to the quilt and finish sewing the binding to the quilt.

11. Turn the binding to the back of the quilt, covering the raw edges. If there is too much batting, trim some away to leave your binding nicely filled. Hand stitch the folded edge of the binding to the back of the quilt.

Embroidery Stitches

Embroidery is fun! Adding embroidery to solid fabrics is especially satisfying. The stitching is a new and delightful addition to any appliqué block.

Embroider your blocks with cotton floss, silk ribbon, or whatever seems appropriate for your quilt. We enjoy the hunt for unusual threads and flosses. Hand-dyed threads are especially fun to work with. Remember to check hand-dyed flosses for colorfastness just as you would fabric.

General Embroidery Instructions

In most cases it is best to embroider the appliqué pieces **before** they are stitched down. Trace the template onto the appliqué fabric. Lightly draw the embroidery design on the fabric. Embroider the appliqué piece **then** cut it out, adding a ³⁄₁₆" turn-under allowance.

In most cases, use two strands of floss for your embroidery. If you want a finer line, use one strand of floss. Create new colors by twisting two different colors of floss together. Use hand-dyed pearl cotton for a bolder presence.

Lazy Daisy Stitch

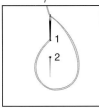 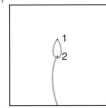 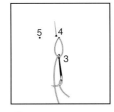 

1. Insert the needle at #1 and back up at #2. Loop the floss below the tip of the needle

2. Pull the stitch through, leaving a loop.

3. Insert the needle at #3, outside the loop. Bring up the needle at #4 to begin the next petal.

4. Make 5 daisy petals. Leave space at the center of the flower for 1 or more French knots.

Random Straight Stitches

1. Fill the area with straight stitches. There is no pattern to the stitches. Vary the length and angle of the stitches.

Zigzag Stitch

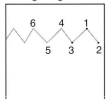 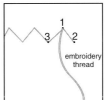 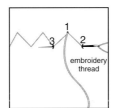 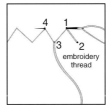

1. Draw the zigzag line.

2. Bring up the thread at #1.

3. Insert the needle at #2 and come up at #3.

4. Insert the needle at #1 and come up at #4. Continue working in this manner.

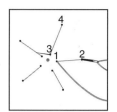

French Knot

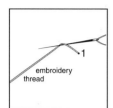

1. Bring up the floss at #1.

2. Wrap the floss around the needle. The more wraps, the bigger the knot.

3. Re-insert the needle at #1, outside of any loops, and pull to the back leaving the French knot on top. Knot off or move to another position and make another knot.

Straight Stitch Flowers

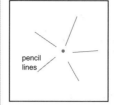
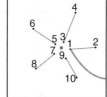

1. Draw flowers on your fabric.

2. Bring up the floss at #1.

3. Insert the needle at #2 and back up at #3. Continue in this manner until the flower petals are complete. Put a French knot in the center of the flower.

Back Stitch

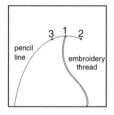
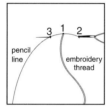
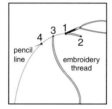

1. Draw the line on the fabric. Bring up the floss at #1.

2. Insert the needle at #2 and come up at #3. Keep the stitches short and uniform.

3. Insert the needle at #1 and come up at #4. Work your way down the line in this manner.

Bullion Knot on a Chain Stitch

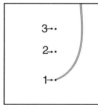
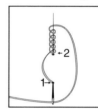
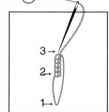

1. Bring the floss to the front at #1.

2. Insert the needle at #1 and back up at #2. Wrap the thread firmly 4 times around the tip of the needle. Hold the wraps with your thumb and pull the needle and thread all the way through.

3. Insert the needle through to the back at #3 and knot the floss.

Blanket Stitch

This stitch is most often done at the edge of an appliqué piece.

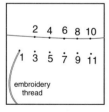
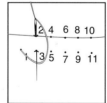
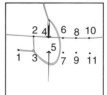

1. Bring up the floss at #1.

2. Insert the needle at #2 and come up at #3. Loop the floss below the tip of the needle.

3. Pull the floss to make an "L" stitch. Continue in this manner along the edge of the appliqué.

Basket Weave

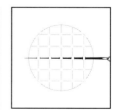
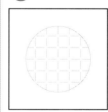
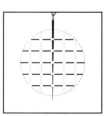

1. Draw the basket weave grid lightly on the fabric.

2. Use 1 strand of floss and a running stitch to sew the horizontal stitches.

3. Sew the vertical stitches.

About the Authors

The Green Country Quilter's Guild in Tulsa, Oklahoma, can be credited for bringing Linda Jenkins and Becky Goldsmith together. Their friendship developed while they worked together on many guild projects and through a shared love for appliqué. This partnership led to the birth of Piece O' Cake Designs in 1994 and survived Linda's move to Pagosa Springs, Colorado, while Becky headed for Sherman, Texas.

Linda owned and managed a beauty salon before she started quilting. Over the years she developed a fine eye for color as a hair colorist and makeup artist. Becky's degree in interior design and many art classes provided a perfect background for quilting. Linda and Becky have shown many quilts and have won numerous awards. Together they make a dynamic quilting duo and love to teach other quilters the joys of appliqué.

In the fall of 2002 Becky and Linda joined the C&T Publishing family, where they continue to produce wonderful books and patterns.

Look for more Piece O' Cake books from C&T Publishing

For information about individual Piece O' Cake Patterns, contact C&T Publishing.

Flowering Favorites

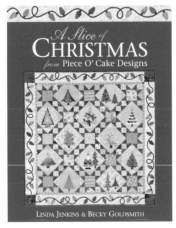

A Slice of Christmas

Contemporary Classics in Plaids & Stripes

The Appliqué Sampler

Index

Projects

Useful Information

Note: Fabrics used in the quilts shown may not be currently available because fabric manufacturers keep most fabrics in print for only a short time.

For more information
ask for a free catalog:
C&T Publishing, Inc.
P.O. Box 1456
Lafayette, CA 94549
800-284-1114
email: ctinfo@ctpub.com
website: www.ctpub.com

Resources

Piece O' Cake Designs
www.Pieceocake.com

Quilting Supplies
Cotton Patch Mail Order
3404 Hall Lane, Dept CTB
Lafayette, CA 94549
800-835-4418   925-283-7883
email: quiltusa@yahoo.com
website: www.quiltusa.com